Chemistry for the Grammar Stage

Teacher Guide

> # THIS PRODUCT IS INTENDED FOR HOME USE ONLY
>
> The images and all other content in this book are copyrighted material owned by Elemental Science, Inc. Please do not reproduce this content on e-mail lists or websites. If you have an eBook, you may print out as many copies as you need for use WITHIN YOUR IMMEDIATE FAMILY ONLY. Duplicating this book or printing the eBook so that the book can then be reused or resold is a violation of copyright.
>
> **Schools and co-ops:** You MAY NOT DUPLICATE OR PRINT any portion of this book for use in the classroom. Please contact us for licensing options at support@elementalscience.com.

Chemistry for the Grammar Stage Teacher Guide

Third Edition (First Printing 2023)
Copyright @ Elemental Science, Inc.
Email: support@elementalscience.com

ISBN #978-1-953490-16-2

Printed in the USA for worldwide distribution

For more copies write to:
Elemental Science
PO Box 79
Niceville, FL 32588
support@elementalscience.com

Copyright Policy

All contents copyright © 2010, 2016, 2020, 2023 by Elemental Science. All rights reserved.

Limit of Liability and Disclaimer of Warranty: The publisher has used its best efforts in preparing this book, and the information provided herein is provided "as is." Elemental Science makes no representation or warranties with respect to the accuracy or completeness of the contents of this book and specifically disclaims any implied warranties of merchantability or fitness for any particular purpose and shall in no event be liable for any loss of profit or any other commercial damage, including but not limited to special, incidental, consequential, or other damages.

Trademarks: This book identifies product names and services known to be trademarks, registered trademarks, or service marks of their respective holders. They are used throughout this book in an editorial fashion only. In addition, terms suspected of being trademarks, registered trademarks, or service marks have been appropriately capitalized, although Elemental Science cannot attest to the accuracy of this information. Use of a term in this book should not be regarded as affecting the validity of any trademark, registered trademark, or service mark. Elemental Science is not associated with any product or vendor mentioned in this book.

Classical SCIENCE Quick Start Guide

In a Nutshell

Students will learn about atoms, the periodic table, and chemistry in the following ways:

✓ Listening to (or reading) **scientific information** from visually appealing encyclopedias.

✓ Watching (and doing) **hands-on science** through demonstrations and activities.

✓ Dictating (or writing down) what they have learned and seen using **notebooking**.

See p. 10 for a list of the topics explored in this program.

What You Need

In addition to this guide, you will need the following:

1. **The student materials** - You can purchase either the *Chemistry for the Grammar Stage Student Workbook* or the *Chemistry for the Grammar Stage Lapbooking Templates*. (Get a glimpse of these options on pp. 8-9.)

2. **The three spines:**
   - *The Usborne Science Encyclopedia* (Usborne Books, 2015 Edition)
   - *The Elements* (DK, 2022 Edition)

   You can also purchase the *Pasteur's Fight Against Microbes* for the scientist biography report in the last week of the Mixtures Unit and *Marie Curie's Search for Radium* for the scientist biography report in the last week of the Acids and Bases Unit. Alternatively, you can check a biography out from your local library. Get links to these books here:

   https://elementalscience.com/blogs/resources/cgs

3. **The demonstration supplies** - See a full list starting on p. 16 or save yourself the time and purchase the *Chemistry for the Grammar Stage Experiment Kit*.

How It Works

Each week you and your early elementary student will do the following

- **Read** the assigned pages with your students and use the included questions to discuss what was read.

- **Do** the weekly demonstration with the students using the scripted introduction, directions, and scripted explanation found in this guide.

- **Write** down what the students have learned and seen in a way that is appropriate for their skills.

You can also add in the optional memory work, library books, and STEAM activities if you want to dig deeper into a topic. For a more detailed explanation of the components in each lesson, we highly recommend checking out the peek inside this program on pp. 6-7 and reading the introduction starting on p. 11. Otherwise, the first lesson begins on p. 22.

Chemistry for the Grammar Stage Teacher Guide Table of Contents

Introduction 2
    Quick Start Guide   3
    A Peek Inside the Grammar Stage Teacher Guide   6
    A Peek Inside the Grammar Stage Student Materials   8
    List of Topics Covered in This Program   10
    Introduction to the Third Edition   11
    Supplies Needed by Week   16

Atoms and Molecules Unit 20
    Week 1: Atoms Lesson Plans   22
    (*Article*) Polar and Non-polar Molecules   27
    Week 2: Molecules Lesson Plans   28
    Week 3: Air Lesson Plans   32
    Week 4: Water Lesson Plans   36

Periodic Table Unit 42
    Week 1: Elements and the Periodic Table Lesson Plans   45
    Week 2: Alkali Metals Lesson Plans   50
    Week 3: Alkaline Earth Lesson Plans   54
    Week 4: Transition Metals Lesson Plans   58
    Week 5: Boron Elements Lesson Plans   62
    Week 6: Carbon Elements Lesson Plans   66
    Week 7: Nitrogen Elements Lesson Plans   70
    Week 8: Oxygen Elements Lesson Plans   74
    Week 9: Halogens Lesson Plans   78
    Week 10: Noble Gases Lesson Plans   82
    Week 11: Lanthanides Lesson Plans   86
    Week 12: Actinides Lesson Plans   90

Physical Changes Unit 96
    Week 1: States of Matter Lesson Plans   98
    Week 2: Changes in State Lesson Plans   102
    Week 3: Liquid Behavior Lesson Plans   106

    Week 4: Gas Behavior Lesson Plans   110

Chemical Changes Unit 116
    Week 1: Bonding Lesson Plans   118
    Week 2: Chemical Reactions Lesson Plans   122
    Week 3: Types of Reactions Lesson Plans   126
    Week 4: Oxidation and Reduction Lesson Plans   130

Mixtures Unit 136
    Week 1: Mixtures Lesson Plans   138
    Week 2: Separating Mixtures Lesson Plans   142
    Week 3: Crystals Lesson Plans   146
    Week 4: Scientist Biography Lesson Plans   150

Acids and Bases Unit 154
    Week 1: Acids and Bases Lesson Plans   156
    Week 2: pH Lesson Plans   160
    Week 3: Neutralization Lesson Plans   164
    (*Article*) Neutralization   168
    Week 4: Scientist Biography Lesson Plans   169

Organic Chemistry Unit 172
    Week 1: Organics Compounds Lesson Plans   174
    Week 2: Alcohols and Detergents Lesson Plans   178
    Week 3: Hydrocarbons Lesson Plans   182
    Week 4: Polymers and Plastics Lesson Plans   186

Appendix Templates 191
    Transition Metal Hunt   193
    Project Record Sheet   194
    Two Days a Week Schedule   195
    Five Days a Week Schedule   196

Glossary 197

Additional Books Listed by Week 205

A Peek Inside the Grammar Stage Teacher Guide

The teacher guide is your go-to resource for creating memorable science lessons!

1. Weekly Topic

Focus on one main idea, with several subtopics, throughout the week. You will learn about these ideas by doing scientific demonstrations, by reading from visually appealing encyclopedias, by recording what the students learned, and by adding other optional activities.

2. Two Scheduling Options

Know what to do when with the two grid-style scheduling options. There are a 2-day-a-week and a 5-day-a-week schedules. These schedules break down the essential work and the optional activities into manageable chunks so that you can proceed with confidence.

3. Reading Assignments

Find two reading options—one for younger students, one for older students—plus discussion questions and optional library books.

4. Memory work

Boost your students' memory of what they have studied with a hallmark of classical education—memory work. These catchy poems share the key facts to remember about the unit's topics.

5. Additional Resources

See options for adding in more information about the weekly topic through children's encyclopedias and library books.

6. Related Scientific Demonstrations

Know what you will need to do a weekly hands-on science activity that coordinates with the topic. This section includes the supplies you will need, along with scripted introductions. The easy-to-follow steps and scripted explanations make it a snap to complete the scientific demonstration. And if your kiddos want more, we have you covered with a related idea to take the science-learning fun even further.

7. Coordinated Unit Projects

Add in a bit of fun with these optional project ideas for the whole unit.

8. Optional STEAM Ideas

Get ideas for additional STEAM activities that relate to the week's topic.

9. Notebooking Assignments

Record what your students have learned with either the student workbook or the optional lapbook. The directions for these options are included for your convenience in the guide. Plus, see which coloring pages coordinate with the week's lesson in this section.

10. Relevant Vocabulary

Build your students' science vocabulary with words relevant to the weekly topic.

11. Review Sheets

See which review sheet to assign —these are found at the back of the student workbook—along with the answers. These sheets can be used as review or as quizzes.

A Peek Inside the Grammar Stage Student Materials

The Student Workbook

Harness the benefits of notebooking with the student workbook.

1. Weekly Notebooking Pages

Record what your students found interesting about the weekly subtopics using a hallmark of classical education—narration. Each of these customized notebooking pages has spaces to write and simple black-line illustrations for the students to color.

2. Simple Demonstration Sheets

Document the hands-on scientific demonstrations you do with simple lab sheets. These include sections for your materials, a simple procedure, your outcome, and the students' insights from the demonstration.

3. Glossary of Terms

Find a student glossary of terms following the weekly sheets. The terms are listed alphabetically with pictures to help your students remember their vocabulary.

4. Memory Work Posters

Help the students work on their memory work with these poster-style sheets. Each poem is in a large, readable font with illustrations related to the information in the poem.

5. Review Sheets

Review what the students have learned with the review sheets found at the back of the student workbook. These can be used as review or quizzes.

Add in the optional lapbooking templates and coloring pages for more fun!

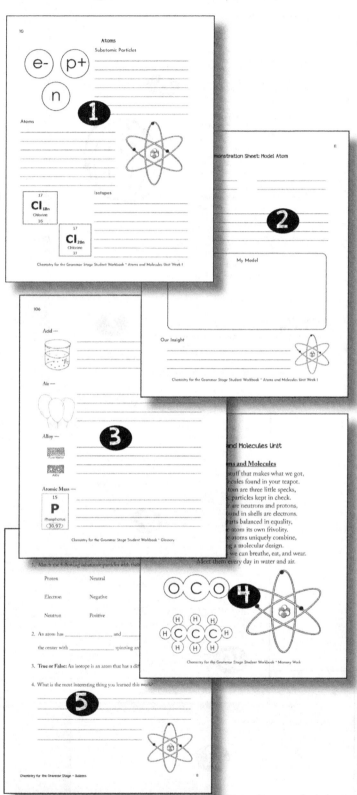

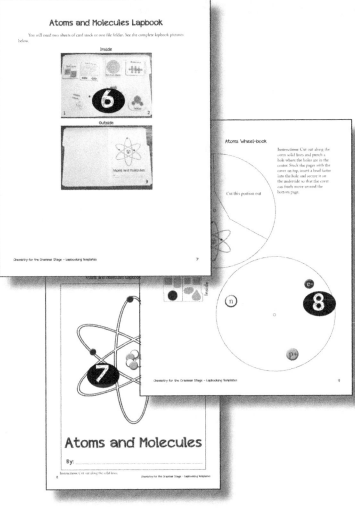

The Lapbooking Templates

Use the lapbooking templates to review the concepts learned, or you can have the student create each one in lieu of completing the student workbook.

6. Lapbook Overview Sheets

Know where to place the mini-books in the lapbook with these overview sheets. You will also find overall directions for completing the lapbook. The specific directions for completing each mini-book are found in the teacher guide.

7. Lapbook Cover

Find a unique cover for each of the suggested lapbooks.

8. Mini-book Templates

Get all the mini-books you will need to complete the suggested lapbooks, along with an exact placement guide. The templates include black-line illustrations and space for narrations.

The Coloring Pages

Use the coloring pages to add a bit of art to your science plans or to engage younger students.

9. Simple Coloring Pages

Color your way through learning about science with these coloring pages. Each page has a large, black-line illustration along with a key fact sentence for the students to learn about the topic. The specific directions for when to use these coloring pages are found in the teacher guide.

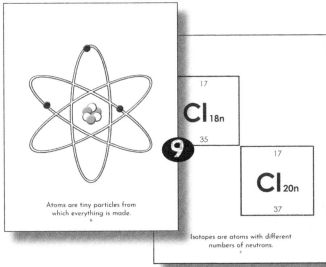

List of Topics Covered in This Program

Atoms and Molecules Unit
- ✓ Atoms
- ✓ Subatomic Particles
- ✓ Molecules
- ✓ Air
- ✓ Water

Periodic Table Unit
- ✓ Elements
- ✓ The Periodic Table
- ✓ Alkali Metals
- ✓ Alkaline Earth Metals
- ✓ Transition Metals
- ✓ Poor Metals
- ✓ Metalloids
- ✓ Nonmetals
- ✓ Halogens
- ✓ Noble Gases
- ✓ Lanthanides
- ✓ Actinides

Physical Changes Unit
- ✓ States of Matter
- ✓ Changes in State
- ✓ Liquid Behavior
- ✓ Gas Behavior

Chemical Changes Unit
- ✓ Bonding (Covalent, Ionic, Metallic)
- ✓ Chemical Reactions
- ✓ Types of Reasons
- ✓ Catalysts
- ✓ Oxidation and Reduction

Mixtures Unit
- ✓ Mixtures
- ✓ Separating Mixtures
- ✓ Crystals
- ✓ Louis Pasteur

Acids and Bases Unit
- ✓ Acids
- ✓ Bases
- ✓ pH
- ✓ Salts
- ✓ Marie Curie

Organic Chemistry Unit
- ✓ Organics Compounds
- ✓ Fats
- ✓ Alcohols
- ✓ Detergents
- ✓ Esters
- ✓ Hydrocarbons
- ✓ Polymers
- ✓ Plastics

Quick Links

The following page contains quick access to the activity links suggested in this guide along with several helpful downloads:

🖱 https://elementalscience.com/blogs/resources/cgs

Introduction to the Third Edition

It has been more than 10 years since the first edition of *Chemistry for the Grammar Stage* was released. With each edition, the format has been refined, but the method has always been based on the same three keys to teaching science:

1. Read about science.
2. Do, or rather play with, science.
3. Write about science.

If you want to learn more about these keys, check out this free conference session:

> *The 3 Keys to Teaching Science* - https://elementalscience.com/blogs/news/3-keys

In this guide are the tools you need to teach science using the Classic Method found in *Success in Science: A Manual for Excellence in Science Education*. This method is loosely based on the ideas for classical science education that are laid out in *The Well-Trained Mind: A Guide to Classical Education at Home* by Jessie Wise and Susan Wise Bauer.

In *Success in Science*, the elementary student is compared to an empty bucket that is waiting to be filled with meaningful information. As such, the goal of this program is to give your elementary student exposure to age-appropriate topics of within the fields of chemistry, building a knowledge base for future studies. The tools you are going to use are weekly scientific demonstrations, reading suggestions, notebooking assignments, additional activities, and more.

Let's take a closer took at what you will find in this guide.

Unit Overview Sheets

Each unit will begin with an overview sheet that shows the resources you will need for the unit, the list of topics, the supplies you will need, the memory work you can use, and the vocabulary you will cover. These are meant to give you a snapshot of the unit. Please feel free to swap the units around, but do keep the weeks within the unit in order as you work through this program.

Weekly Lesson Schedules

Each week's lesson will begin with a breakdown of what your week could look like. There are two potential schedules for you to give an idea of how you could schedule each week—one that breaks the assignments over 2 days, and one that breaks these assignments over 5 days. Each of these schedules has three sections to reflect the three keys to teaching science—read, do, and write (more about these in a moment). Optional assignments are in italics so you can easily see what is required and what can be used as gravy on the week's science meal.

You can choose to use these schedules as your guide or create your own using the two schedule templates on pp. 195-196 of the appendix of this guide. You could also create a list schedule or mark the lesson plans with a checkmark or date when you do the assignment.

In other words, you, the teacher, have complete freedom in what you would like to use to present and explore the concepts each week. Please treat the schedules and information in this guide as tools to teach science, not as weekly task masters.

Read – Information Gathering

Reading Assignments

The first things you will see in the "Read" section are the reading assignments. These come from the following three encyclopedias:

- 📖 *The Usborne Science Encyclopedia* (Usborne Books, 2015 Edition)
- 📖 *The Elements* (DK, 2022 Edition)

These resources are essential for completing this program. You can often use older editions because they are virtually the same on the inside. (**Note –** *At this point, the idea is that you read the assigned pages to your students. Here is a helpful podcast to determine if your students can handle reading science on their own: Should I read science aloud or not?* https://elementalscience.com/blogs/podcast/79)

After the assigned pages, you will find questions to ask your students after you have finished the reading selections. Here is an example:

? What is the point of these questions?

The point is to get your students to think about the information that was read to them. This seems like an extra, unnecessary step, but please don't skip these questions as they are designed to help your students get ready for the writing portion. Here is another helpful podcast about discussion times:

🎧 Don't skip that science discussion time: https://elementalscience.com/blogs/podcast/53

{Optional} Memory Work

Next up in the "Read" section is the unit's optional memory work. An elementary student is capable of memorizing information and you can use this spongelike ability to have the students memorize basics facts related to chemistry through simple poems. Remember that these poems are included as a resource for you to augment students' learning experiences and are not required to use this program successfully.

{Optional} Additional Resources

The final item in the "Read" section is a list of optional additional resources. First are several alternative encyclopedias, in case your student has a hard time (or an easy time) with the one from the reading assignments. Here is a list of all of the *optional* encyclopedias that are scheduled:

- 📖 *The Usborne Children's Encyclopedia* (2014 Edition)
- 📖 *The DK Children's Encyclopedia* (2022 Edition)
- 📖 *Basher Science: Chemistry* (2010 Edition)
- 📖 *Basher Science: The Complete Periodic Table* (2015 Edition)
- 📖 *The Periodic Table by Sean Callery* (Scholastic, 2017 Edition)

You *do not* need to purchase these encyclopedias to complete this program. They are there as options to explore the topics deeper or to use as alternatives.

Finally, you will see a list of potential library books. These books are meant to be checked out from the library in case you decide that you would like to dig a little deeper into the topics. They are not necessary to the success of this program. Because every library is different, the books listed may not be available in your area. If that is the case, simply look up the topic in your local library's system. A complete list of all the suggested books can be found in the appendix pp. 205-206.

Do – Demonstration and Activities

Scientific Demonstrations

The bulk of the items in the "Do" section have to relate to the week's scientific demonstration. These generally use easy-to-find materials and tie into what is being studied. At this age, you will be the driving force behind these demonstrations, meaning that you will be the one in control, and the students will be watching and participating when necessary. (**Note –** *If you want to read more about the differences between demonstrations and experiments, check out the following article: https://elementalscience.com/blogs/news/89905795-scientific-demonstrations-or-experiments*)

You will find several sections for the scientific demonstration:

- ❑ The Demonstration Title and Supplies
- ❑ The Instructions (*including a scripted introduction and detailed instructions*)
- ❑ The Explanation (*including the expected results and a scripted explanation*)

All scripted text, introductions, and explanations will be in this font.

- ❑ Ideas to Take the Demonstration Further

These demonstrations are designed to provide a beginner's look at the scientific method and how scientific tests work. Even so, it is not necessary to ask the students to predict the outcome of the demonstration because they have no knowledge base to determine what the answer should be. However, if your students enjoy predicting or they are able to tell you what will happen, please feel free to let them do so.

{Optional} Unit Projects and Weekly Activities

The final two items in the "Do" section are packed with STEAM activities that coordinate with each lesson. These are definitely optional, but they can be used to add in fun and deepen understanding. Here is a podcast to help you decide if you should use these activities:

- 🖱 Do you need to bother with the "extras" for science? https://elementalscience.com/blogs/podcast/22

The pages and pictures needed for the unit projects are included in the student workbook, whereas the directions for creating the projects are found in this guide. The weekly activities include crafts and other activities that can enhance the students' learning time. There are no sheets to record these additional activities in the student workbook. However, I have included a project record sheet template on p. 194 of the appendix of this guide.

Write - Notebooking

Writing Assignments

In the first part of the "Write" section, you will be asking the students to narrate and record what they have learned from the reading assignments in a student workbook. (**Note** - *We have put together a complete workbook for your students to record what they did—the Chemistry for the Grammar Stage Student Workbook, which you can peek inside on p. 8 of this guide. It contains all the pages you will need to complete the narrations, demonstration reports, and multi-week projects, along with memory work posters, alphabetical sheets for the student glossary, and review sheets. The student workbook gives the students the ability to create a lasting memory of their first journey through chemistry.*)

For younger students, you can have them dictate what they have learned to you, and then you write this into the student workbook. You can also have the students copy their narration into the workbook. You should expect only three to four sentences from a 3rd- or 4th-grade student. Here is a sample of what the students could write for week one of the Atoms and Molecules unit:

> *There are three subatomic particles – protons, neutrons, and electrons.*
> *Protons and neutrons live in the nucleus of an atom.*
> *Electrons fly around the nucleus.*
> *Protons are positively charged and electrons are negatively charged.*

When you are done writing, you can have the students color the provided picture on the narration page.

Here are a podcast and a video that will help you understand a bit more about how this process works:

- How do we narrate and what to expect - https://elementalscience.com/blogs/podcast/78
- Writing in Science: The Elementary Years - https://youtu.be/BrunFyeHhlQ

We also offer two other consumable options for the students—lapbooking templates and coloring pages. These are optional, but they can be used as review or in place of the student workbook.

- *Chemistry for the Grammar Stage Lapbooking Templates*
- *Chemistry for the Grammar Stage Coloring Pages*

Both of these are also scheduled in under the "Writing Assignments" section. You can peek inside these two resources on p. 9 of this guide.

Demonstration Sheets

The demonstration sheets are assigned in the "Do" section, but because they include writing, the explanation for how to use them is here. Each one of the scientific demonstrations has a corresponding sheet in the student workbook.

These demonstration sheets include four sections:

1. The "Our Tools" section is for the materials that were used during the demonstration.
2. The "Our Method" section is for a brief description of what was done during the scientific demonstration. This should be in the students' words.

3. The "Our Outcome" section is for what the students observed during the demonstration.
4. The "Our Insight" section is for what the students learned from the scientific demonstration.

Any time you see a box for a picture on the demonstrations sheet, you can have the students draw what happened, or you can take a picture of the demonstration and glue it in the box. For younger students, you can do the writing for them on the demonstration sheets.

Vocabulary

Next in the "Write" section, you will find the week's vocabulary. You can go over these words orally or have the students copy the definitions into the glossary at the rear of the student workbook. If you want to have the students practice looking up the definitions, you can use the included glossary of the terms on pp. 199-202 of this guide.

{Optional} Review Sheets

The last part of the "Write" section assigns a weekly review sheet. These sheets are found at the back of the student workbook. Although these review sheets are not essential, they are helpful in assessing how much the students are retaining. You can also use these review sheets as quizzes. The correct answers for the review sheets are found at the end of the lesson's materials.

Final Thoughts

Our goal at Elemental Science is to provide you with the information you need to be successful in your quest to educate your students in the sciences at home, which is why I encourage you to contact us with any questions or problems that you might have concerning this program at support@elementalscience.com. I, or a member of our team, will be more than happy to answer them as soon as we are able. I hope that you enjoy this year with *Chemistry for the Grammar Stage*!

- Paige Hudson

Supplies Needed by Week

Atoms and Molecules Unit

Week	Supplies needed
1	4 Pipe cleaners, Round beads in three different colors (at least 3 of each color)
2	Jar with lid, Water, Food Coloring
3	Candle, Match, Clear glass bottle
4	Cup, Water, Salt

Periodic Table Unit

Week	Supplies needed
1	LEGO® bricks in a variety of colors and sizes, Paper, Pen
2	3 Cups, Water, Food coloring, Salt, Instant-read thermometer
3	Epsom salts, Ammonia, Water, Clear cup
4	Steel wool, Vinegar, Jar with lid
5	Alum powder, Ammonia, Clear jar, Water
6	Sugar, Baking soda, Rubbing alcohol, Sand, Aluminum pie pan (or other dish you can throw away), Match
7	Can of dark cola soda, Glass, Dirty pennies
8	Candle, Match, Glass jar
9	Small piece of potato, Small piece of bread, Small piece of fruit, Iodine swab
10	Helium-filled balloon, Scissors
11	3 Cups, 3 Pencils, 3 Clear liquids (i.e., water, alcohol, and corn syrup)
12	Bite-sized food, such as raisins or cereal puffs, Timer

Physical Changes Unit

Week	Supplies needed
1	3 Balloons, Ice, Water
2	Orange juice, Cup
3	Pepper, Dish soap, Bowl, Water
4	Empty aluminum can, Bowl, Hot water, Ice, Tongs, Pan

Supplies Needed by Week

Chemical Changes Unit

Week	Supplies needed
1	Salt, Magnifying glass, Warm water, Cup, Spoon
2	Shallow dish, Paper towel, Bowl, Vinegar, Pennies
3	Baking soda, Vinegar, Water, Epsom salts, 2 Cups
4	Apple, Cotton ball, Lemon juice

Mixtures Unit

Week	Supplies needed
1	Clear glass, Warm water, Powdered sugar
2	Washable markers, Coffee filter, Shallow dish or pan
3	Glass jar, Pencil, Pipe cleaners, Borax, Hot water
4	*No supplies needed.*

Acids and Bases Unit

Week	Supplies needed
Unit Prep*	Head of purple cabbage, Knife, Pot, Distilled water, Strainer, Clear glass jar or plastic container, Coffee Filters, Bowl, Cookie Sheet, Scissors, Plastic baggie
1	Water, Lemon juice, Cabbage indicator, Glass, Tablespoon
2	Cabbage paper, Vinegar, Ammonia, Jars with lids
3	Vinegar, Baking soda, Water, Cabbage juice, Cabbage paper, 2 Clear cups, Eyedropper
4	*No supplies needed.*

Organic Chemistry Unit

Week	Supplies needed
1	Construction paper, 6 Types of food (Cheese, Fruit, Yogurt, Chips, Muffin, Vegetable), Marker
2	Cotton ball, Vanilla Extract
3	Large clear glass bowl, Vegetable Oil, Water, Plastic spoon, Cotton balls, Polyester felt square
4	Vegetable oil, Cornstarch, Water, Food coloring, Plastic bag, Eyedropper

Chemistry for the Grammar Stage Teacher Guide ~ Supply List

Chemistry for the Grammar Stage

Atoms and Molecules Unit

Atoms and Molecules Unit Overview
(4 weeks)

Books Scheduled
 📖 *Usborne Science Encyclopedia*

{Optional Encyclopedias}
 📖 *Basher Science Chemistry*
 📖 *Usborne Children's Encyclopedia*
 📖 *DK Children's Encyclopedia*

Sequence for Study
 ↷ Week 1: Atoms
 ↷ Week 2: Molecules
 ↷ Week 3: Air
 ↷ Week 4: Water

Atoms and Molecules Unit Memory Work

Atoms and Molecules
Atoms are the stuff that makes what we got,
Forming molecules found in your teapot.
Inside the atom are three little specks,
Subatomic particles kept in check.
At the center are neutrons and protons,
Spinning around in shells are electrons.
All three parts, balanced in equality,
Give the atom its own frivolity.
One or more atoms uniquely combine,
Creating a molecular design.
These molecules we can breathe, eat, and wear.
Meet them every day in water and air.

Supplies Needed for the Unit

Week	Supplies needed
1	4 Pipe cleaners, Round beads in three different colors (at least 3 of each color)

2	Jar with lid, Water, Food Coloring
3	Candle, Match, Clear glass bottle
4	Cup, Water, Salt

Unit Vocabulary
1. **Electron** – A negatively charged particle in an atom.
2. **Proton** – A positively charged particle in an atom.
3. **Neutron** – A neutral particle in an atom.
4. **Isotope** – An atom that has a different number of neutrons and so has a different mass number from the other atoms of an element.
5. **Electron Shell** – The region around an atom's nucleus in which a certain number of electrons can reside.
6. **Molecule** – A substance made up of two or more atoms that are chemically bonded.
7. **Air** – A mixture of gases that forms a protective layer around the Earth.
8. **Hard Water** – Water that contains a lot of dissolved minerals.

Week 1: Atoms Lesson Plans

2-Days-a-week Schedule

	Day 1	Day 2
Read	☐ Read "Atomic Structure, part 1 and part 2" ☐ {Choose one or more of the additional resources to read from this week}	☐ Read "Isotopes and Atomic Theory" ☐ {Work on memorizing the "Atoms and Molecules" poem}
Do	☐ {Play the Atoms and Isotopes Game or Complete the Atoms and Molecules Poster}	☐ Do the Scientific Demonstration: Model Atom
Write	☐ Add information about atoms and subatomic particles to the students' notebook or lapbook ☐ Define electron, proton, neutron, and isotope	☐ Add information about isotopes to the students' notebook or lapbook ☐ Complete the demonstration sheet ☐ {Work on the Atoms and Molecules Weekly Review Sheet 1}

5-Days-a-week Schedule

	Day 1	Day 2	Day 3	Day 4	Day 5
Read	☐ Read "Atomic Structure, part 1"	☐ Read "Atomic Structure, part 2"	☐ {Work on memorizing the "Atoms and Molecules" poem}	☐ Read "Isotopes and Atomic Theory"	☐ {Choose one or more of the additional resources to read from this week}
Do	☐ {Make an Atomic Cookie}	☐ {Complete the Atoms and Molecules Poster}	☐ Do the Scientific Demonstration: Model Atom	☐ {Play the Atoms and Isotopes Game}	
Write	☐ Add information about subatomic particles to the students' notebook or lapbook	☐ Add information about atoms to the students' notebook or lapbook	☐ Complete the demonstration sheet ☐ Define electron, proton, neutron, and isotope	☐ Add information about isotopes to the students' notebook or lapbook	☐ {Work on the Atoms and Molecules Weekly Review Sheet 1}

{These assignments are optional.}

Read - Information Gathering

Reading Assignments

- ❑ *Usborne Science Encyclopedia* p. 10 "Atomic Structure, part 1"
    - **?** What are the three subatomic particles?
    - **?** Do you remember what the charge of an electron is? The charge of a proton is? The charge of a neutron is?
- ❑ *Usborne Science Encyclopedia* p. 11 "Atomic Structure, part 2"
    - **?** What is an atom?
    - **?** Can you describe what an atom look likes?
- ❑ *Usborne Science Encyclopedia* p. 13 "Isotopes and Atomic Theory"
    - **?** What is an isotope?

{Optional} Memory Work

- This week, begin memorizing the *Atoms and Molecules* poem. (SW p. 120)

{Optional} Additional Resources

Encyclopedias
- *Basher Science Chemistry* p. 26 "Atom," p. 28 "Isotope"
- *Usborne Children's Encyclopedia* p. 186 (section entitled "What is an atom?")
- *DK Children's Encyclopedia* p. 187 "Atoms"

Library Books
- *What Are Atoms? (Rookie Read-About Science)* by Lisa Trumbauer
- *Atoms and Molecules (Building Blocks of Matter)* by Richard and Louise Spilsbury
- *Atoms (Simply Science)* by Melissa Stewart

Do - Demonstration and Activities

Demonstration - Model Atom

You will need the following:
- ✓ 4 Pipe cleaners
- ✓ Round beads in three different colors (at least 3 of each color)

Demonstration Instructions

1. Read the following introduction to the students.

    Never trust an atom.

    They make up everything!

    Seriously, atoms are tiny particles that are so small that we can't see them, but they make up everything we see. Inside these atoms, we find three different pieces called subatomic particles. Protons are positively-charged particles found the nucleus or center of the atom. They like to hang out with neutrally-charged particles called neutrons in the nucleus. Then, flying around the outside of the nucleus are the electrons, which are negatively charged. Different combinations of these subatomic particles make up different atoms, and these atoms make up everything we see! In today's demonstration, we are going to make a model of the atom that we can see.

2. Have the students select which beads will be electrons, protons, and neutrons.
3. Next, have them string three protons beads and three neutrons beads on one of the pipe cleaners, alternating between the two. Once done, have the students wrap this portion of the pipe cleaner into a ball to form a nucleus, leaving a straight end to connect to the electron rings they will make in the next step.
4. Then, have the students place one electron bead on a pipe cleaner and twist the pipe cleaner closed to form a ring. Repeat this process two more times so that they have three electron rings.
5. Finally, fit the rings inside each other and then hang the nucleus ball in the center, using the pipe cleaner tail left in step two to attach the nucleus and hold the rings together. (*See image for reference.*)
6. Read the demonstration explanation to the students, take a picture of their atoms, and have the students complete the demonstration sheet on SW p. 11.

Demonstration Explanation

The purpose of this demonstration was for the students to see what an atom looks like. As they are finishing their observations, ask the following questions:

? Can you point to the electrons? The protons? The neutrons?

{Optional} Take the Demonstration Further

Have the students make a fruit atom model. In the center of a plate, have the students build a mound of raspberries and grapes for the protons and neutrons in the nucleus. Then, they can roll blueberries in a circle around the nucleus for the electrons. Once, they are done playing, let the students gobble their atoms up!

{Optional} Unit Project

✂ **Atoms and Molecules Poster** – During this unit, the students will create a poster about atoms and molecules, giving them a visual representation of the basics of chemistry. The poster will have three main sections: subatomic particles, atoms and elements, and molecules. This week, have the students add the electron, proton, and neutron to the "subatomic particle" section. They can draw or paint circles with charges for each or use pompoms. Then, have them use the same circles or pompoms to represent an atom on the left-hand side of the "atoms and elements" section. (*See the included image.*) After the students finish the artwork, have them write a sentence or two about each subatomic particle. (*This has been done for you in the SW on p. 8.*)

{Optional} Projects for This Week
- ✂ **Atomic Cookie** – Make some subatomic cookies with your students using a sugar cookie, white icing, and three different colors of M&M's. See the following website for directions:
  - 🖑 http://technoprairie.blogspot.com/2009/02/atomic-cookies.html
- ✂ **Atoms and Isotopes Game** – Have the students play an atoms and isotopes game. You can get directions for this game from the following blog post:
  - 🖑 http://elementalscience.com/blogs/science-activities/60317571-free-chemistry-game

Write – Notebooking
Writing Assignments
- ☐ **Student Workbook** – Have the students dictate, copy, or write two to four sentences on subatomic particles, atoms, and isotopes on *Chemistry for the Grammar Stage Student Workbook* (SW) p. 10.
- ☐ **{Optional} Lapbooking Templates** – Have the students begin the Atoms and Molecules lapbook by cutting out and coloring the cover on p. 8 of *Chemistry for the Grammar Stage Lapbooking Templates* (LT).
- ☐ **{Optional} Lapbooking Templates** – Have the students complete the Atoms wheel-book on LT p. 9. Have them cut along the solid lines, punch a hole in the center, and use a brad fastener to fasten the two circles together. Have the students write their electron narration to the left of the picture, their proton narration above the picture, and their neutron narration to the right of the picture. Finally, have them glue their mini-book into the lapbook.
- ☐ **{Optional} Lapbooking Templates** – Have the students complete the Isotopes shutterfold book on LT p. 10. Have them cut out and fold the template. Have the students color the pictures on the cover. Have them write their narration about the isotopes inside the mini-book. Then, have them glue the mini-book into the lapbook.
- ☐ **{Optional} Coloring Pages** – Have the students color the following pages from *Chemistry for the Grammar Stage Coloring Pages* (CP): Atoms CP p. 6, Isotopes CP p. 7.

Vocabulary
Have the students look up and copy the definitions for the following words:
- ✎ **Electron** – A negatively charged particle in an atom. (SW p. 109)
- ✎ **Proton** – A positively charged particle in an atom. (SW p. 115)
- ✎ **Neutron** – A neutral particle in an atom. (SW p. 113)

◇ **Isotope** – An atom that has a different number of neutrons and so has a different mass number from the other atoms of an element. (SW p. 112)

{Optional} Weekly Review Sheet
↳ "Atoms and Molecules Weekly Review Sheet 1" on SW p. 135.
   Answers:
   1. Positive, Negative, Neutral
   2. Protons, Neutrons, Electrons
   3. True
   4. Answers will vary

Polar and Non-polar Molecules

There are two different types of molecules: polar and nonpolar. In a nutshell, polar molecules have a charge, whereas nonpolar molecules do not.

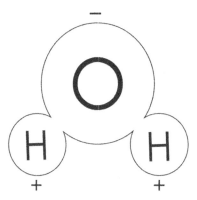

A polar molecule has two ends, just like a magnet: one end of the molecule is positive, and the other end of the molecule is negative. Water is an example of a polar molecule. Polar molecules are attracted to other polar molecules.

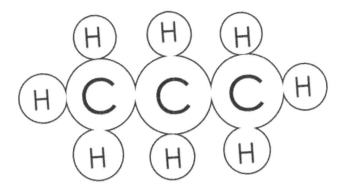

A nonpolar molecule does not have a positive or a negative end. These molecules are known as neutral molecules. Oil is an example of a nonpolar molecule. Nonpolar molecules are attracted to other nonpolar molecules.

In solutions, we say that like dissolves like. Polar molecules can dissolve other polar molecules. Nonpolar molecules can dissolve nonpolar molecules. Polar and nonpolar molecules do not dissolve in each other, which is why oil and water do not mix.

Week 2: Molecules Lesson Plans

	2-Days-a-week Schedule	
	Day 1	**Day 2**
Read	❏ Read "Molecules, part 1 and part 2" ❏ *{Choose one or more of the additional resources to read from this week}*	❏ Read "Polar or Nonpolar Molecules" ❏ *{Work on memorizing the "Atoms and Molecules" poem}*
Do	❏ *{Have a Polarity Race or Complete the Atoms and Molecules Poster}*	❏ Do the Scientific Demonstration: Moving Molecules
Write	❏ Add information about molecules to the students' notebook or lapbook ❏ Define electron shell and molecule	❏ Add information about molecules to the students' notebook or lapbook ❏ Complete the demonstration sheet ❏ *{Work on the Atoms and Molecules Weekly Review Sheet 2}*

	5-Days-a-week Schedule				
	Day 1	**Day 2**	**Day 3**	**Day 4**	**Day 5**
Read	❏ Read "Molecules, part 1"	❏ Read "Molecules, part 2"	❏ *{Work on memorizing the "Atoms and Molecules" poem}*	❏ Read "Polar or Nonpolar Molecules"	❏ *{Choose one or more of the additional resources to read from this week}*
Do	❏ *{Make a few LEGO Molecules}*	❏ *{Complete the Atoms and Molecules Poster}*	❏ Do the Scientific Demonstration: Moving Molecules	❏ *{Have a Polarity Race}*	
Write	❏ Add information about molecules to the students' notebook or lapbook	❏ Add information about molecules to the students' notebook or lapbook	❏ Complete the demonstration sheet ❏ Define electron shell and molecule	❏ Add information about molecules to the students' notebook or lapbook	❏ *{Work on the Atoms and Molecules Weekly Review Sheet 2}*

Read - Information Gathering

Reading Assignments

- ❑ *Usborne Science Encyclopedia* p. 14 "Molecules, part 1"
    - **?** What is a molecule?
    - **?** Do you remember how many electrons fit in the first shell? The second shell? The third shell?
- ❑ *Usborne Science Encyclopedia* p. 15 "Molecules, part 2"
    - **?** Do you remember one or two examples of molecules?
    - **?** What are two ways, or models, of showing molecules?
- ❑ "Polar and Nonpolar Molecules" article p. 27 of this guide
    - **?** What is a nonpolar molecule?
    - **?** What is a polar molecule?

Additional Explanantion: Molecules or Compounds

Molecules are formed when two or more atoms join together. Compounds are formed when two or more elements join together. For example H_2 (hydrogen gas) is a molecule because two atoms of hydrogen are joined together. However, because there is only one type of element present, H_2 is not a compound. On the other hand, H_2O (water) is a molecule because the three atoms, one oxygen atom and two hydrogen atoms, have been joined together to form it. It is also a compound because it contains two different elements, hydrogen and oxygen. So, all compounds are molecules, but not all molecules are compounds.

{Optional} Memory Work

- 🗣 This week, begin memorizing the *Atoms and Molecules* poem. (SW p. 120)

{Optional} Additional Resources

Encyclopedias
- 📖 *Basher Science Chemistry* p. 32 "Molecules"
- 📖 *Usborne Children's Encyclopedia* pp. 186-187 "Atoms and Molecules"
- 📖 *DK Children's Encyclopedia* p. 184 "Chemistry"

Library Books
- 📖 *Atoms and Molecules (Building Blocks of Matter)* by Richard and Louise Spilsbury
- 📖 *Atoms and Molecules (Why Chemistry Matters)* by Molly Aloian
- 📖 *Atoms and Molecules (My Science Library)* by Tracy Nelson Maurer

Do - Demonstration and Activities

Demonstration - Moving Molecules

You will need the following:
- ✓ Jar with lid, Water, Food coloring

Demonstration Instructions

1. Read the following introduction to the students.

   Last week we learned about atoms, the tiny particles that make up everything. These atoms like to get together to form molecules. Even though we can't see them, these molecules are always doing something! In today's demonstration, we are going to see molecules in motion.

2. Have the students fill the jar almost to the top with room-temperature water and drop several drops of food coloring into the water.
3. Observe what happens within the first 30 seconds and draw what you see in the box on the demonstration sheet on SW p. 13.
4. Wait an hour and observe the jar again. Draw what you see in the box on the demonstration sheet.
5. Read the demonstration explanation to the students and have the students complete the demonstration sheet.

Demonstration Explanation

The purpose of this demonstration was for the students to visualize molecules in motion. When they are done, read the following to them:

   In the beginning, we could clearly see the drops of food coloring moving through the water. After an hour, the whole cup was full of colored water. This is because the atoms and molecules that make up these two liquids are in constant motion. Even though we can't see them moving, the water molecules are bumping into the food coloring molecules. Eventually, the two will be evenly mixed in the jar. This type of molecular movement is called diffusion.

{Optional} Take the Demonstration Further

Have the students look at how temperature affects molecular motion by repeating the demonstration with a glass each of ice-cold and hot-to-the-touch water. (*They should see that the food coloring molecules move much faster in the hot-to-the-touch water.*)

{Optional} Unit Project

✂ **Atoms and Molecules Poster** – This week, have the students add a picture of molecules to the "molecules and compounds" section of their poster. This can be as simple as the written formula for water (H_2O) or methane (CH_4) or as complicated as a drawing of one of the molecules they saw in their readings. After the students finish the artwork, have them write a sentence or two about molecules.

{Optional} Projects for This Week

✂ **LEGO Molecules** – Have the students make molecules models out of LEGOs using the examples from the following pin:
   🔗 https://www.pinterest.com/pin/192036371586132562/

✂ **Polarity Race** – Have the students have a molecule race using a polar substance (water) and a nonpolar one (wax paper). Use an eyedropper to sprinkle a drop of water at the end of a wax paper sheet in front of each student. Then, give each of the students a straw and have them blow through it to move their water "molecule" drop to the finish line at the other end of the wax paper.

Write – Notebooking

Writing Assignments

- ☐ **Student Workbook** – Have the students dictate, copy, or write two to four sentences on electron shells, molecules, and nonpolar and polar molecules on SW p. 12. (**Note** – *The information for the electron shells is not super clear. You can share with the students that the first shell can contain two electrons, the second shell can contain eight electrons, and the third shell generally carries eight electrons, but can carry as many as 18 for certain atoms.*)
- ☐ **{Optional} Lapbooking Templates** – Have the students work on the Electron Shell Diagram on LT p. 10. Have the students cut out the sheet, color the shells different colors, and add the information they have learned about how many electrons the first three shells can carry. Finally, have them glue their sheets into their lapbooks.
- ☐ **{Optional} Lapbooking Templates** – Have the students work on the Molecules tab-book on LT p. 11. Have the students write the definition of a molecule on the definition page and then add any molecules they have learned about to the samples page. Set the mini-book aside and save it for next week.
- ☐ **{Optional} Coloring Pages** – Have the students color the following pages: Electron Shells CP p. 8, Molecules CP p. 9, Polar and Nonpolar Molecules CP p. 10.

Vocabulary

Have the students look up and copy the definitions for the following words:
- ✎ **Electron Shell** – The region around an atom's nucleus in which a certain number of electrons can reside. (SW p. 109)
- ✎ **Molecule** – A substance made up of two or more atoms that are chemically bonded. (SW p. 113)

{Optional} Weekly Review Sheet

- ✤ "Atoms and Molecules Weekly Review Sheet 2" on SW p. 136.

    Answers:
    1. 2, 8, 8 to 18
    2. False (*A molecule can be made up of more than one element.*)
    3. Charged, Not charged
    4. Answers will vary

Week 3: Air Lesson Plans

	2-Days-a-week Schedule	
	Day 1	**Day 2**
Read	❏ Read "Air, part 1" ❏ {Choose one or more of the additional resources to read from this week}	❏ Read "Air, part 2" ❏ {Work on memorizing the "Atoms and Molecules" poem}
Do	❏ {Play the Air Game or Complete the Atoms and Molecules Poster}	❏ Do the Scientific Demonstration: Fresh Air
Write	❏ Add information about air to the students' notebook or lapbook ❏ Define air	❏ Add information about air to the students' notebook or lapbook ❏ Complete the demonstration sheet ❏ {Work on the Atoms and Molecules Weekly Review Sheet 3}

	5-Days-a-week Schedule				
	Day 1	**Day 2**	**Day 3**	**Day 4**	**Day 5**
Read	❏ Read "Air, part 1"	❏ {Work on memorizing the "Atoms and Molecules" poem}	❏ Read "Air, part 2"	❏ {Choose one or more of the additional resources to read from this week}	❏ {Choose one or more of the additional resources to read from this week}
Do	❏ {Play the Air Game}	❏ Do the Scientific Demonstration: Fresh Air	❏ {Do the Fire Extinguisher Activity}	❏ {Complete the Atoms and Molecules Poster}	
Write	❏ Add information about air to the students' notebook or lapbook	❏ Complete the demonstration sheet	❏ Add information about air to the students' notebook or lapbook	❏ Define air	❏ {Work on the Atoms and Molecules Weekly Review Sheet 3}

Read – Information Gathering

Reading Assignments

- ❏ *Usborne Science Encyclopedia* p. 62 "Air, part 1"
   - **?** What is air?
   - **?** Do you remember the two main gases found in air?
   - **?** What is oxygen essential for?
   - **?** What do plants and animals do with oxygen?
- ❏ *Usborne Science Encyclopedia* p. 63 "Air, part 2"
   - **?** What is carbon dioxide?
   - **?** What do plants and animals do with carbon dioxide?
   - **?** Can you tell me two of the six noble gases found in air?

{Optional} Memory Work

- This week, begin memorizing the *Atoms and Molecules* poem. (SW p. 120)

{Optional} Additional Resources

Encyclopedias
- *Basher Science Chemistry* p. 96 "Air," p. 110 "Oxygen," p. 112 "Carbon Dioxide"
- *DK Children's Encyclopedia* p. 269 "Atmosphere"

Library Books
- *Air Is All Around You (Let's-Read-and-Find... Science 1)* by Franklyn M. Branley
- *Air: Outside, Inside, and All Around (Amazing Science)* by Darlene R. Stille

Do – Demonstration and Activities

Demonstration – Fresh Air

You will need the following:
- ✓ Candle
- ✓ Match
- ✓ Clear glass bottle

Demonstration Instructions

1. Read the following introduction to the students.

   Last week, we saw how molecules are in constant motion. This week we are learning about a very vital molecular mixture–air! Air is a mixture of gases that surrounds our planet. And, like the molecules in last week's demonstration, these gases are always in motion. But what happens when we keep new, fresh air from coming into a space? In today's demonstration, we are going to see how important fresh air is to a fire, which needs the oxygen found in air to burn.

2. (**Adults Only**) Light the candle using the match.

3. Have the students observe that the candle burns well.
4. Then, cover the candle with an upside glass jar so that no more fresh air can get to the candle.
5. Have the students observe what happens to the candle and write it down on the demonstration sheet on SW p. 15.
6. Read the demonstration explanation to the students and have the students complete the demonstration sheet.

Demonstration Explanation

The purpose of this demonstration was for the students to see why fresh air is important to a fire. When they are done, read the following to them:

> The candle burned quite well when it was uncovered. This is because fire on a candle needs the oxygen found in air to keep burning. When we covered it with the glass jar, the candle burned for a bit and then went out. This is because the fire used up all the oxygen found in the trapped air in the bottle. Once the oxygen is gone, the candle stops burning. That's why fire needs fresh air to burn and why firefighters will often smother a fire with water or chemicals to put it out.

{Optional} Take the Demonstration Further

Have the students repeat the demonstration with an open tube. If you don't have a glass tube that is open on both ends and will cover the candle, you can use a can. Simply use a can opener to cut both ends of the candle off. Then, relight the candle and cover it with the tube. (*This time, the candle should keep burning for much longer and may never go out.*)

{Optional} Unit Project

- **Atoms and Molecules Poster** – This week, have the students add a picture of oxygen to the "atoms and elements" section and carbon dioxide to the "molecules and compounds" section of their poster. After the students finish the artwork, have them write a sentence or two about what they have added.

{Optional} Projects for This Week

- **Air Game** – Have the students play a game with air. You will need a balloon for this activity. Blow up the balloon, sharing with the students that air is what fills the balloon. Then, hit the balloon back and forth to each other. The goal of the game is to keep the balloon from touching the ground. See how many times you can go back and forth without doing so!
- **Fire Extinguisher** – Have the students test how carbon dioxide puts out a fire. You will need a candle, a bottle, baking soda, and vinegar. The directions for this activity can be found in the *Usborne Science Encyclopedia* on p. 63.

Write - Notebooking

Writing Assignments
- ☐ **Student Workbook** – Have the students dictate, copy, or write two to four sentences on on air, oxygen, and carbon dioxide on SW p. 14.
- ☐ **{Optional} Lapbooking Templates** – Have the students add carbon dioxide to the samples page of their molecule tab-book. Set the mini-book aside and save it for next week.
- ☐ **{Optional} Lapbooking Templates** – Have the students complete the Air mini-book on LT p. 12. Have them cut out and fold the template. Have the students color the pictures on the cover. Have them write their narration about the air inside the mini-book. Then, have them glue the mini-book into the lapbook.
- ☐ **{Optional} Coloring Pages** – Have the students color the following pages: Air CP p. 11.

Vocabulary
Have the students look up and copy the definitions for the following words:
- **Air** – A mixture of gases that forms a protective layer around the Earth. (SW p. 106)

{Optional} Weekly Review Sheet
- "Atoms and Molecules Weekly Review Sheet 3" on SW p. 137.
    Answers:
    1. Nitrogen, Oxygen
    2. Life
    3. Oxygen, Carbon dioxide, Carbon dioxide, Oxygen
    4. Answers will vary

Week 4: Water Lesson Plans

2-Days-a-week Schedule

	Day 1	Day 2
Read	❏ Read "Water, part 1 and part 2" ❏ {Choose one or more of the additional resources to read from this week}	❏ Read "The Water Cycle" ❏ {Work on memorizing the "Atoms and Molecules" poem}
Do	❏ {Do the Hard Water Activity or Complete the Atoms and Molecules Poster}	❏ Do the Scientific Demonstration: Disappearing Salt
Write	❏ Add information about water to the students' notebook or lapbook ❏ Define hard water	❏ Add information about water to the students' notebook or lapbook ❏ Complete the demonstration sheet ❏ {Work on the Atoms and Molecules Weekly Review Sheet 4}

5-Days-a-week Schedule

	Day 1	Day 2	Day 3	Day 4	Day 5
Read	❏ Read "Water, part 1"	❏ Read "Water, part 2"	❏ {Work on memorizing the "Atoms and Molecules" poem}	❏ Read "The Water Cycle"	❏ {Choose one or more of the additional resources to read from this week}
Do	❏ {Make some Water Art}	❏ {Do the Hard Water Activity}	❏ Do the Scientific Demonstration: Disappearing Salt	❏ {Complete the Atoms and Molecules Poster OR View the Water Cycle}	
Write	❏ Add information about water to the students' notebook or lapbook	❏ Define hard water ❏ Add information about water to the students' notebook or lapbook	❏ Complete the demonstration sheet	❏ Add information about water to the students' notebook or lapbook	❏ {Work on the Atoms and Molecules Weekly Review Sheet 4}

Read – Information Gathering

Reading Assignments

- ❑ *Usborne Science Encyclopedia* p. 72 "Water, part 1"
    - **?** What is the most abundant compound on earth?
    - **?** What two elements make up water?
    - **?** Do you remember what water is called when it heats up? When it freezes?
- ❑ *Usborne Science Encyclopedia* p. 73 "Water, part 2"
    - **?** Can you tell me why is water a good solvent?
    - **?** What makes water hard?
    - **?** What makes water soft?
- ❑ *Usborne Science Encyclopedia* p. 74 "The Water Cycle"
    - **?** What is the water cycle?

{Optional} Memory Work

- This week, begin memorizing the *Atoms and Molecules* poem. (SW p. 120)

{Optional} Additional Resources

Encyclopedias

- *Basher Science Chemistry* p. 108 "Water"
- *Usborne Children's Encyclopedia* p. 14 "The Weather" (*This page has information on the water cycle.*)
- *DK Children's Encyclopedia* pp. 100-101 "Water," p. 99 "Water Cycle"

Library Books

- *Water, Water Everywhere (Reading Rainbow Book)* by Cynthia Overbeck Bix
- *Water* by Frank Asch
- *Water: Up, Down, and All Around (Amazing Science)* by Natalie M. Rosinsky

Do – Demonstration and Activities

Demonstration – Disappearing Salt

You will need the following:
- ✓ Cup
- ✓ Water
- ✓ Salt

Demonstration Instructions

1. Read the following introduction to the students.

    This week, we are wrapping up our look at atoms and molecules with a look at water. Water is a compound that contains hydrogen and oxygen. It's one of the most common compounds on Earth. It has some special properties that can make it appear magical! In today's demonstration, we are going to watch what happens when salt meets water.

2. Have the students fill the cup about halfway with warm water.
3. Then, have them add a teaspoon of salt and stir it around several times.
4. Have the students observe what happens and write what they see on the demonstration sheet on SW p. 17.
5. Read the demonstration explanation to the students and have the students complete the demonstration sheet.

Demonstration Explanation

The purpose of this demonstration was for the students to see how water easily dissolves a substance. When they are done, read the following to them:

Did you see what happened to the salt? It quickly disappeared after a few stirs—this isn't magic, it's science! Remember that water molecules have a slight charge. This slight charge allows for ionic compounds, like salt, to easily dissolve in water. For this reason, water is known as the universal solvent.

{Optional} Take the Demonstration Further

Have the students repeat the process using sugar to see if the results vary.

{Optional} Unit Project

- **Atoms and Molecules Poster** – This week, have the students add a picture of hydrogen to the "atoms and elements" section and water to the "molecules and compounds" section of their poster. After the students finish the artwork, have them write a sentence or two about what they have added.

{Optional} Projects for This Week

- **Water Art** – Have the students paint with watercolors! As they create their pictures, discuss the fact that they are able to paint with the colors because water is such a good solvent.
- **Hard water** – Make a jar of hard water and observe its sudsing capabilities. You will need plaster of Paris, water, liquid soap, and a jar with a lid. Have the students mix 1 TBSP of plaster of Paris with 1 cup of water in the jar. Mix well. Add several drops of liquid soap, cover, and shake the jar for about 30 seconds and observe the bubbles formed. (*The water in the jar is hard and should not create very many bubbles. If you want to compare it with soft water, repeat the activity, only this time use Epsom salts instead of the plaster of Paris.*)
- **Water Cycle** – If you haven't studied the water cycle in a previous program, have the students view the following interactive water cycle:
  - https://water.usgs.gov/edu/watercycle-kids-beg.html

Write – Notebooking

Writing Assignments

- ☐ **Student Workbook** – Have the students dictate, copy, or write two to four sentences on water and the water cycle on SW p. 16.
- ☐ **{Optional} Lapbooking Templates** – Have the students add water to the samples page of their molecule tab-book. Set the mini-book aside and save it for next week.
- ☐ **{Optional} Lapbooking Templates** – Have the students complete the Water mini-book on LT p. 13. Have them cut out and fold the template. Have the students color the pictures on the cover. Have them write their narration about water inside the mini-book. Then, glue the mini-book into the lapbook.
- ☐ **{Optional} Lapbooking Templates** – Have the students finish their lapbook. Have them cut out and color the *Atoms and Molecules* poem on LT p. 14. Once they are done, have them glue the sheet into their lapbook.
- ☐ **{Optional} Coloring Pages** – Have the students color the following pages: Water CP p. 12, Water Cycle CP p. 13.

Vocabulary

Have the students look up and copy the definitions for the following words:

- **Hard Water** – Water which contains a lot of dissolved minerals. (SW p. 111)

{Optional} Weekly Review Sheet

- "Atoms and Molecules Weekly Review Sheet 4" on SW p. 138.

    Answers:
    1. Water
    2. More, Less
    3. True
    4. Answers will vary

Chemistry for the Grammar Stage

Periodic Table Unit

Periodic Table Unit Overview
(12 weeks)

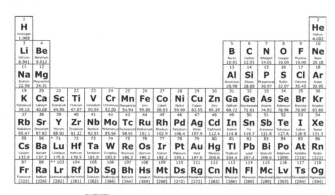

Books Scheduled
📖 *DK Eyewitness The Elements*

{Optional Encyclopedias}
📖 *Basher Science Complete Periodic Table*
📖 *Scholastic's The Periodic Table*
📖 *Usborne Science Encyclopedia*

Sequence for Study
- **Week 1:** Elements and the Periodic Table
- **Week 2:** Alkali Metals
- **Week 3:** Alkaline Earth Metals
- **Week 4:** Transition Metals
- **Week 5:** Boron Elements
- **Week 6:** Carbon Elements
- **Week 7:** Nitrogen Elements
- **Week 8:** Oxygen Elements
- **Week 9:** Halogens
- **Week 10:** Noble Gases
- **Week 11:** Lanthanides
- **Week 12:** Actinides

Periodic Table Poems to Memorize

<u>The Periodic Table</u> *(Author Unknown)*
Each element has a spot on the Periodic Table,
Whether metal or gas, radioactive or stable.
You can find out its number, its symbol, its weight,
And from its position, its physical state.

Elements lined up in columns and rows,
The reason for this order, as each chemist knows,
Is that atoms are made up of still smaller bits,
(Figuring this out tested scientists' wits!)

In the nucleus, protons and neutrons are found,
And a cloud of electrons is buzzing around.
First take one proton, put in its place;

Now you have hydrogen, the simplest case.

Add two neutrons and one more proton,
And suddenly, the hydrogen's gone!
Now you have helium, quite different stuff…
You get the picture; I've said enough.

These tiny particles: they're like building blocks
That make people and buildings, flowers and rocks.
They create all of the elements we find
In everyday things of every kind!

Supplies Needed for the Unit

Week	Supplies needed
1	LEGO® bricks in a variety of colors and sizes, Paper, Pen
2	3 Cups, Water, Food coloring, Salt, Instant-read thermometer
3	Epsom salts, Ammonia, Water, Clear cup
4	Steel wool, Vinegar, Jar with lid
5	Alum powder, Ammonia, Clear jar, Water
6	Sugar, Baking soda, Rubbing alcohol, Sand, Aluminum pie pan (or other dish you can throw away), Match
7	Can of dark cola soda, Glass, Dirty pennies
8	Candle, Match, Glass jar
9	Small piece of potato, Small piece of bread, Small piece of fruit, Iodine swab
10	Helium-filled balloon, Scissors
11	3 Cups, 3 Pencils, 3 Clear liquids (i.e., water, alcohol, and corn syrup)
12	Bite-sized food, such as raisins or cereal puffs, Timer

Unit Vocabulary

1. **Atomic Number** – The number of protons in the nucleus of an atom.
2. **Atomic Mass** – The average mass number of the atoms in a sample of an element.
3. **Elements** – A substance made up of one type of atom, which cannot be broken down by chemical reaction to form a simpler substance.
4. **Chemical Symbol** – A shorthand way of representing a specific element in formulae and equations.

5. **Periodic Table** – A systematic arrangement of the elements in order of increasing atomic number.
6. **Reactive** – The tendency of a substance to react with other substances.
7. **Metal** – The largest class of elements; they are usually shiny and solid at room temperature.
8. **Alloy** – A mixture of two or more metals or a metal and a nonmetal.
9. **Metalloid** – An element that shares some of the properties of metals and nonmetals.
10. **Nonmetal** – A class of elements that can be nonshiny solids or gases.
11. **Essential Element** – An element that is essential to life on earth, such as carbon, hydrogen, nitrogen, or oxygen.
12. **Oxidation** – A chemical reaction in which a substance combines with oxygen.
13. **Ion** – An atom or group of atoms that has become charged by gaining or losing one or more electrons.
14. **Inert** – An element that is completely nonreactive.
15. **Refraction** – The bending of light as it passes through a different medium.
16. **Radioactive Decay** – The process by which a nucleus ejects particles through radiation to become the nucleus of a series of different elements until stability is reached.

Week 1: Elements and the Periodic Table Lesson Plans

	2-Days-a-week Schedule	
	Day 1	**Day 2**
Read	❏ Read "What is an element?" ❏ {Choose one or more of the additional resources to read from this week}	❏ Read "The Periodic Table" ❏ {Work on memorizing the "Periodic Table" poem}
Do	❏ {Learn the "Periodic Table" Song or Complete the Atoms and Molecules Poster}	❏ Do the Scientific Demonstration: Table Sorting
Write	❏ Add information about the elements to the students' notebook or lapbook ❏ Define atomic number, atomic mass, element, chemical symbol, and periodic table	❏ Add information about the periodic table to the students' notebook or lapbook ❏ Complete the demonstration sheet ❏ {Work on the Periodic Table Weekly Review Sheet 1}

	5-Days-a-week Schedule				
	Day 1	**Day 2**	**Day 3**	**Day 4**	**Day 5**
Read	❏ Read "What is an element?"	❏ Read "The Periodic Table"	❏ {Work on memorizing the "Periodic Table" poem}	❏ {Choose one or more of the additional resources to read from this week}	❏ {Choose one or more of the additional resources to read from this week}
Do	❏ {Create an Element Report}	❏ {Learn the "Periodic Table" Song}	❏ Do the Scientific Demonstration: Model Atom	❏ {Play the Periodic Table Game}	❏ {Complete the Atoms and Molecules Poster}
Write	❏ Add information about the elements to the students' notebook or lapbook	❏ Add information about the periodic table to the students' notebook or lapbook	❏ Complete the demonstration sheet	❏ Define atomic number, atomic mass, element, chemical symbol, and periodic table	❏ {Work on the Periodic Table Weekly Review Sheet 1}

{These assignments are optional.}

Read – Information Gathering

Reading Assignments

- ❑ *DK Eyewitness The Elements* pp. 4-5 "What is an element?"
    - **?** What is every element made up of?
    - **?** What are the three primary states that an element can exist in?
    - **?** Do you remember two of the six of the elements that make up the human body?
- ❑ *DK Eyewitness The Elements* pp. 8-9 "The Periodic Table"
    - **?** What is the periodic table?
    - **?** Who designed the periodic table?
    - **?** Do you remember what the difference between groups and periods is?

Additional Explanantion: Element or Atom

How do atoms and elements differ? Elements are substances that are made up of one type of atom, while atoms are the smallest particles of an element that retain the chemical properties of the element. In other words, an element is composed of one or more of the same type of atom. So, when you hold a lump of iron ore, you are holding the element iron, which contains billions of iron atoms.

{Optional} Memory Work

- This week, begin memorizing the *Periodic Table* poem. (SW p. 121)

{Optional} Additional Resources

Encyclopedias
- *Basher Science Periodic Table* p. 18 "Elements," p. 6 "Periodic Table"
- *Scholastic's The Periodic Table* pp. 8-9 "What is an element?," pp. 14-15 "The Periodic Table"
- *Usborne Science Encyclopedia* pp. 24-25 "The Elements," pp. 28-29 "The Periodic Table"

Library Books
- *The Elements (True Books)* by Matt Mullins
- *Elements and Compounds (Building Blocks of Matter)* by Louise and Richard Spilsbury
- *The Mystery of the Periodic Table (Living History Library)* by Benjamin D. Wiker, Jeanne Bendick, and Theodore Schluenderfritz
- *The Periodic Table (True Books: Elements)* by Salvatore Tocci

Do – Demonstration and Activities

Demonstration – Table Sorting

You will need the following:
- ✓ LEGO® bricks in a variety of colors and sizes (*You can also used stuffed animals, buttons, beads, or any other object with different sizes and colors if you don't have any LEGO bricks.*)

- ✓ Paper
- ✓ Pen

Demonstration Instructions

1. Read the following introduction to the students.

    As scientists discovered more and more elements, they needed a way to organize them. Many scientists had ideas about how to do this, but one scientist is credited with the organizational system we still use today. Dmitri Mendeleev created the earliest version of the periodic table. It doesn't look exactly like what we will learn about in this unit, but his version has a lot of similarities! In today's demonstration, you are going to create your own mini-version of a periodic table.

2. Gather the LEGO bricks in an unorganized pile. Draw a 4 by 6 grid on the piece of paper. (*If you are using larger objects to sort, such as stuffed animals, you can create this grid on the floor with masking tape.*)
3. Explain to the students that you are going to make a periodic table of LEGO bricks. In your table, the bricks are going to get bigger as you go down the grid and darker as you go across. (*See the included grid for visual explanation.*)
4. Have the students sort the LEGO bricks by size and color onto the grid.
5. When they are done, have the students dictate, copy, or write one to four sentences and add a picture of their finished table on the demonstration sheet on SW p. 23.

	White	Yellow	Red	Blue	Brown	Black
smallest						
largest						

Demonstration Explanation

The point of this demonstrations is for the students to see the order that exists in the arrangement of the elements in the periodic table. As they are finishing their observations, ask the following questions:

> **?** Is there anything in the way you organized the LEGO bricks that you would change?

{Optional} Take the Demonstration Further

Have the students create another table for different objects.

{Optional} Unit Project

✂ **Atoms and Molecules Poster** – This week, have the students add an element, complete with its atomic number, atomic mass, and symbol, to the "atoms and elements" section of the poster from the last unit. After the students finish the artwork, have them write a sentence or two about elements.

{Optional} Projects for This Week

- ✂ **Element Report** – Have the students flip through *DK Eyewitness The Elementals* or *Basher's Science The Periodic Table* and choose an element to learn more about. Have them read the selected page and then create a poster for the element. The poster should include the basic chemical information for the element (i.e., its atomic number, atomic mass, and symbol), along with where the element is found, several uses for it, and its physical appearance. (**Note** – *You can also can have them do a bit of additional online research for this project.*)
- ✂ **Periodic Table Song** – Have the students listen to the "Periodic Table" Song as many times as they need to until they are able to memorize the elements:
  - 🖱 https://www.youtube.com/watch?v=rz4Dd1I_fX0

  You can also use flash cards to help memorize the elements of the periodic table.
- ✂ **Periodic Table Game** – Have the students play a game of Periodic Table Battleship! You can see directions and print out game sheets at the following website:
  - 🖱 http://teachbesideme.com/periodic-table-battleship/

Write – Notebooking

Writing Assignments

- ☐ **Student Workbook** – Have the students dictate, copy, or write two to four sentences on elements and the periodic table on *Chemistry for the Grammar Stage Student Workbook* (SW) p. 22. (**Note** – You can also have the students label the element image with atomic number, atomic mass, chemical name, and chemical symbol.)

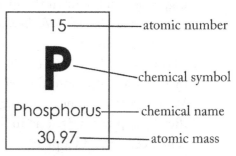

- ☐ **{Optional} Lapbooking Templates** – Have the students begin the Periodic Table lapbook by cutting out and coloring the cover on p. 16 of *Chemistry for the Grammar Stage Lapbooking Templates* (LT).
- ☐ **{Optional} Lapbooking Templates** – Have the students work on the Elements Diagram on on LT p. 17. Have the students cut out the sheet and label the atomic number, atomic mass, chemical name, and chemical symbol on the element. Finally, have them glue the sheet into their lapbook.
- ☐ **{Optional} Lapbooking Templates** – Have the students work on the Periodic Table Book on LT p. 18. Have the students cut out, fold the template, and color the picture on the cover. Have the students write their narration about the periodic table inside the mini-book. Then glue the mini-book into the lapbook.
- ☐ **{Optional} Coloring Pages** – Have the students color the following pages from *Chemistry for the Grammar Stage Coloring Pages* (CP): Periodic Table CP p. 14.

Vocabulary

Have the students look up and copy the definitions for the following words:
- **Atomic Number** – The number of protons in the nucleus of an atom. (SW p. 107)
- **Atomic Mass** – The average mass number of the atoms in a sample of an element. (SW p. 106)
- **Element** – A substance made up of one type of atom, which cannot be broken down by chemical reaction to form a simpler substance. (SW p. 110)
- **Chemical Symbol** – A shorthand way of representing a specific element in formulae and equations. (SW p. 108)
- **Periodic Table** – A systematic arrangement of the elements in order of increasing atomic number. (SW p. 114)

{Optional} Weekly Review Sheet

- "Periodic Table Weekly Review Sheet 1" on SW p. 139.

    Answers:
    1. See the labeled-element picture under discussion questions.
    2. True
    3. False (*An element is made up of one single type of atom.*)
    4. Answers will vary

Week 2: Alkali Metals Lesson Plans

2-Days-a-week Schedule		
	Day 1	Day 2
Read	☐ Read "Hydrogen" and "Alkali Metals, Part 1" ☐ {Choose one or more of the additional resources to read from this week}	☐ Read "Alkali Metals, Part 2" ☐ {Work on memorizing the "Periodic Table" poem}
Do	☐ {Do the Sodium Reaction or Add the group to the Periodic Table Poster}	☐ Do the Scientific Demonstration: Which one freezes first?
Write	☐ Add information about alkali metals to the students' notebook or lapbook ☐ Define reactive	☐ Add information about alkali metals to the students' notebook or lapbook ☐ Complete the demonstration sheet ☐ {Work on the Periodic Table Weekly Review Sheet 2}

5-Days-a-week Schedule					
	Day 1	Day 2	Day 3	Day 4	Day 5
Read	☐ Read "Hydrogen"	☐ Read "Alkali Metals, Part 1"	☐ {Work on memorizing the "Periodic Table" poem}	☐ Read "Alkali Metals, Part 2"	☐ {Choose one or more of the additional resources to read from this week}
Do	☐ {Learn about Hindenburg Hydrogen}	☐ {Eat an Alkali Metal}	☐ Do the Scientific Demonstration: Model Atom	☐ {Do the Sodium Reaction}	☐ {Add the group to the Periodic Table Poster}
Write	☐ Add information about alkali metals to the students' notebook or lapbook	☐ Add information about alkali metals to the students' notebook or lapbook	☐ Complete the demonstration sheet ☐ Define reactive	☐ Add information about alkali metals to the students' notebook or lapbook	☐ {Work on the Periodic Table Weekly Review Sheet 2}

Read – Information Gathering

Reading Assignments
- ❏ *DK Eyewitness The Elements* pp. 12-13 "Hydrogen"
  - **?** What are some characteristics of hydrogen?
  - **?** Do you remember two places that you can find hydrogen?
- ❏ *DK Eyewitness The Elements* pp. 14-15 "Alkali Metals, Part 1"
  - **?** What are some of the characteristics of alkali metals?
  - **?** Can you describe some of the characteristics of sodium?
- ❏ *DK Eyewitness The Elements* pp. 16-17 "Alkali Metals, Part 2"
  - **?** Can you describe some of the characteristics of potassium?
  - **?** Which alkali metal was your favorite?

{Optional} Memory Work
- This week, continue to work on memorizing the *Periodic Table* poem. (SW p. 121)

{Optional} Additional Resources
Encyclopedias
- *Scholastic's The Periodic Table* pp. 24-29 "Alkali Metals," pp. 20-21 "Hydrogen"
- *Basher Science The Periodic Table* p. 10 "Alkali Metals," p. 8 "Hydrogen," p. 14 "Sodium"

Library Books
- *The Alkali Metals: Lithium, Sodium, Potassium, Rubidium, Cesium, Francium* by Kristi Lew
- *Hydrogen and the Noble Gases (True Books: Elements)* by Salvatore Tocci
- *Hydrogen: Running on Water (Energy Revolution)* by Niki Walker
- *Sodium (Elements)* by Anne O'Daly
- *Sodium (True Books: Elements)* by Salvatore Tocci

Do – Demonstration and Activities

Demonstration – Which one freezes first?
You will need the following:
- ✓ 3 Cups
- ✓ Water
- ✓ Food coloring
- ✓ Salt
- ✓ Instant-read thermometer

Demonstration Instructions
1. Read the following introduction to the students.

   Last week, we learned about elements and how they are arranged in the periodic table. This week, we are going to look at the first group in the periodic table: the alkali metals. This group of six metals react very quickly with water, but they form many stable compounds that we use in our everyday life, such as sodium chloride, which is also known as table salt. In today's demonstration, we

are going to see the power of this alkali-metal compound.
2. Have the students begin by labeling the cups #1 to #3. Then, add a half cup of water to each of the cups.
3. Next, do the following:
   ✓ To cup #1, add several drops of food coloring and mix well.
   ✓ To cup #2, add one tablespoon of salt and stir until completely dissolved.
   ✓ To cup #3, add nothing.
4. Have the students take the initial temperature of the cups and place each one in the freezer.
5. Over the next 2 hours, have them check the cups every 30 minutes to observe what is happening and take the temperature of each cup. Each time, have the students record the temperature in the box on the demonstration sheet on SW p. 25.
6. After 2 hours, have them add their final observations to the demonstration sheet.

Demonstration Explanation

The purpose of this demonstration was for the students to understand how salt, which contains the alkali metal sodium, affects freezing temperatures. When they are done, read the following to them:

> We saw that cup #1 and cup #2 froze at about the same time, but cup #3 took quite a bit longer to freeze. The strange part was that all three cups were around the same temperature each time. This is because salt, which is the alkali-metal containing compound sodium chloride, lowers the freezing point of water. This means that water with salt in it will remain a liquid for longer than plain water because the point at which salt water will freeze is lower than 32°F. Food coloring has no effect on the freezing temperature of water, so it will freeze at the same temperature as the plain water.

{Optional} Take the Demonstration Further

Once all of your cups have frozen, have the students take them out of the freezer and see which one melts the quickest. You can do this by setting each cup on the counter or by heating them in a pan. The students should see that cup #3 (the one with the salt) melts quicker for the same reasons in the explanation. This is why we use salt to melt ice on the driveway during the winter.

{Optional} Unit Project

✂ **Periodic Table Poster** – Over the next several weeks, the students will make a poster of the periodic table as they learn about the different groups. You can use the blank sheet found in the student workbook on p. 20, or you can make your own wall-sized periodic table. The pictures for the groups of the periodic table are found in the SW Appendix on p. 129 and p. 131. This week, have the students cut out the picture of the alkali metal group, color it red, and add it to the blank table.

{Optional} Projects for This Week

✂ **Eat an Alkali Metal** – Have the students eat the alkali metal potassium found in a banana!

Potassium is an element important for life. It helps our nerves function properly and aids the brain in transmitting messages to our muscles.

✂ **Hindenburg Hydrogen** – Have the students learn about the *Hindenburg*, which was an air ship filled with hydrogen. You can read the following books with your students:
- 📖 *You Wouldn't Want to Be on the Hindenburg!* by Ian Graham
- 📖 *The Hindenburg Disaster (True Books: Disasters)* by Peter Benoit

Please preview these books to make sure that they are appropriate for your students.

✂ **Sodium Reaction** – Have the students learn about the chemistry of another sodium compound in your kitchen, baking soda (a.k.a. sodium bicarbonate). Add 1 tablespoon of baking soda to a cup. Then, have the students add a few drops of white vinegar and observe what happens! (*This is the classic acid (vinegar) and base (baking soda) reaction. The bubbles you see are a release of the energy and the products from the reaction—carbon dioxide gas, sodium acetate, and water.*)

Write – Notebooking

Writing Assignments

- ☐ **Student Workbook** – Have the students dictate, copy, or write two to four sentences on hydrogen and alkali metals on SW p. 24.
- ☐ **{Optional} Lapbooking Templates** – Have the students work on the Central Periodic Table on LT p. 20. Have the students cut out the picture of the periodic table template and glue it into their lapbook. Then, color the alkali metals red.
- ☐ **{Optional} Lapbooking Templates** – Have the students work on the Alkali Flip-book on LT p. 21. Have the students cut along the solid lines and color the group on the cover red. Next, have the students write several characteristics of alkali metals on the characteristics tab, as well as several facts about hydrogen and sodium on the respective tabs. Then, have them line the pages up and staple the sheets together. Finally, have them glue the flip-book into the lapbook.
- ☐ **{Optional} Coloring Pages** – Have the students color the following pages: Alkali Metals CP p. 15.

Vocabulary

Have the students look up and copy the definition for the following word:

- **Reactive** – The tendency of a substance to react with other substances. (SW p. 116)

{Optional} Weekly Review Sheet

- "Periodic Table Weekly Review Sheet 2" on SW p. 114.

    Answers:
    1. True
    2. Gas
    3. Found in lots of common componds; Very reactive; Light grey metal
    4. Answers will vary

Week 3: Alkaline Earth Lesson Plans

2-Days-a-week Schedule		
	Day 1	**Day 2**
Read	❏ Read "Alkaline Earth Metals, Part 1" ❏ {Choose one or more of the additional resources to read from this week}	❏ Read "Alkaline Earth Metals, Part 2" ❏ {Work on memorizing the "Periodic Table" poem}
Do	❏ {Eat Magnesium or Add the group to the Periodic Table Poster}	❏ Do the Scientific Demonstration: Magnesium Solutions
Write	❏ Add information about alkaline earth metals to the students' notebook or lapbook	❏ Add information about alkaline earth metals to the students' notebook or lapbook ❏ Complete the demonstration sheet ❏ {Work on the Periodic Table Weekly Review Sheet 3}

5-Days-a-week Schedule					
	Day 1	**Day 2**	**Day 3**	**Day 4**	**Day 5**
Read	❏ Read "Alkaline Earth Metals, Part 1"	❏ Read "Alkaline Earth Metals, Part 2"	❏ {Work on memorizing the "Periodic Table" poem}	❏ {Choose one or more of the additional resources to read from this week}	❏ {Choose one or more of the additional resources to read from this week}
Do	❏ {Eat Magnesium}	❏ {Dissolve some Calcium}	❏ Do the Scientific Demonstration: Magnesium Solutions	❏ {Learn about Alkaline Earth Fireworks}	❏ {Add the group to the Periodic Table Poster}
Write	❏ Add information about alkaline earth metals to the students' notebook or lapbook	❏ Add information about alkaline earth metals to the students' notebook or lapbook	❏ Complete the demonstration sheet		❏ {Work on the Periodic Table Weekly Review Sheet 3}

Read – Information Gathering

Reading Assignments

- ❏ *DK Eyewitness The Elements* p. 18-19 "Alkaline Earth Metals, Part 1"
  - **?** What are some of the characteristics of alkaline earth metals?
  - **?** Can you describe some of the characteristics of magnesium?
- ❏ *DK Eyewitness The Elements* p. 20-21 "Alkaline Earth Metals, Part 2"
  - **?** Can you describe some of the characteristics of calcium?
  - **?** Which alkaline earth metal was your favorite?

{Optional} Memory Work
- This week, continue to work on memorizing the *Periodic Table* poem. (SW p. 121)

{Optional} Additional Resources

Encyclopedias
- *Basher Science Complete Periodic Table* p. 22 "Alkaline Earth Metals," p. 26 "Magnesium," p. 28 "Calcium"
- *Scholastic's The Periodic Table* pp. 34-35 "Alkaline Earth Metals," p. 37 "Magnesium," pp. 40-41 "Calcium"

Library Books
- *The Alkaline Earth Metals: Beryllium, Magnesium, Calcium, Strontium, Barium, Radium (Understanding the Elements of the Periodic Table)* by Bridget Heos
- *Calcium (True Books: Elements)* by Salvatore Tocci
- *Magnesium (The Elements)* by Colin Uttley

Do – Demonstration and Activities

Demonstration – Magnesium Solutions

You will need the following:
- ✓ Epsom salts
- ✓ Ammonia
- ✓ Water
- ✓ Clear Cup

Demonstration Instructions

1. Read the following introduction to the students.

   Last week, we learned about alkali metals. This week, we are going to look at their close cousins, the alkaline earth metals. These elements are less reactive than the alkali metals, but they do make up a lot of common chemicals. The alkaline earth metals were first discovered in the Earth's crust. In today's demonstration, we are going to see one of those alkaline earth compounds.

2. Have the students fill the cup about halfway with warm water.
3. Then, add a teaspoon of Epsom salts and stir until it's dissolved.
4. Next, pour in two teaspoons of ammonia, but DO NOT stir.
5. Let the jar sit for five minutes, and observe what happens.
6. Have the students draw what they see on the demonstration sheet on SW p. 27 before reading the demonstration explanation to them.

Demonstration Explanation

The purpose of this demonstration was for the students to create an alkaline-earth-metal-containing compound, one with magnesium. When they are done, read the following to them:

> After five minutes, we saw a milky, white substance appear in the jar. This substance is magnesium hydroxide, which does not dissolve in water. Magnesium hydroxide is a compound that contains an alkaline earth metal, magnesium. If we let the cup sit without touching it for about 30 minutes or longer, the white substance will settle into a layer that sits on top of the water. In this demonstration, a chemical reaction created a new compound, and that new compound did not dissolve in water, so it precipitated or came out of the solution.

{Optional} Take the Demonstration Further

Have the students make another magnesium solution that forms crystals. You will need Epsom salts, water, and a small jar. Have the students mix a third of a cup of Epsom salts with a half of a cup of warm water. Stir to dissolve, and place the jar in the refrigerator where it can sit undisturbed. Check the jar after a few hours and observe what has happened. (*The students should see crystals have formed at the bottom of the jar. These are magnesium sulfate crystals, which are the main chemical in Epsom salts. When the students added the Epsom salts to the water, they were creating a magnesium sulfate solution. As the water cooled, the magnesium sulfate came out of the solution to form crystals once more.*)

{Optional} Unit Project

✂ **Periodic Table Poster** – This week, have the students cut out the picture of the alkaline earth metal group, color it orange, and add it to the blank table in the student workbook on p. 20 or on your wall-sized periodic table. The pictures for the groups of the periodic table are found in the SW Appendix on p. 129.

{Optional} Projects for This Week

✂ **Alkaline Earth Fireworks** – Several of the alkaline earth elements are responsible for giving fireworks their colors. Learn more about the chemistry of fireworks in the following video:
  🔗 https://www.youtube.com/watch?v-nPHcgSuII_M

✂ **Eat Magnesium** – Have the students eat their veggies! Magnesium is one of the elements that is essential to keep our body working properly. We can get the magnesium we need from green veggies, but unfortunately when you boil veggies too long a lot of the beneficial magnesium compounds come out. However, if you add a pinch of baking soda the magnesium will stay put. This week, boil two batches of the green veggies of your choice: broccoli or spinach are good options. Add a pinch of baking soda to one of the pots and have the students observe the difference.

- **Dissolve Calcium** – Have the students dissolve some calcium! You will need an egg, white vinegar, and a clear glass. Place the egg in the glass and cover it with vinegar. Cover the glass, set it aside, and wait for twenty-four hours. The next day, pour out the vinegar and observe the changes to the shell. (*The shell of the egg contains calcium, which is dissolved by the acid in vinegar.*)

Write - Notebooking

Writing Assignments
- **Student Workbook** – Have the students dictate, copy, or write one to four sentences about alkaline earth metals on SW p. 26.
- **{Optional} Lapbooking Templates** – Have the students work on the Central Periodic Table. This week, have the students color the alkaline earth metals orange.
- **{Optional} Lapbooking Templates** – Have the students work on the Alkaline Earth Flip-book on LT p. 21. Have the students cut along the solid lines and color the group on the cover orange. Next, have the students write several characteristics of alkaline earth metals on the characteristics tab as well as several facts about magnesium and calcium on the respective tabs. Then, line the pages up and staple the sheets together. Finally, glue the flip-book into the lapbook.
- **{Optional} Coloring Pages** – Have the students color the following pages: Alkaline Earth Metals CP p. 16.

Vocabulary
- There are no vocabulary words for this week.

{Optional} Weekly Review Sheet
- "Periodic Table Weekly Review Sheet 3" on SW p. 141.
    Answers:
    1. Soft metals; React easily
    2. False (*Magnesium is a solid metal that burns with a bright white light.*)
    3. Students' answers can include the following: bones, teeth, hard water, limestone, cement, and chalk
    4. Answers will vary

Week 4: Transition Metals Lesson Plans

	2-Days-a-week Schedule	
	Day 1	**Day 2**
Read	☐ Read "Transition Metals, Part 1 & 2" ☐ {Choose one or more of the additional resources to read from this week}	☐ Read "Transition Metals, Part 3" ☐ {Work on memorizing the "Periodic Table" poem}
Do	☐ {Go on a Transition Metal Hunt or Add the group to the Periodic Table Poster}	☐ Do the Scientific Demonstration: Rusted
Write	☐ Add information about transition metals to the students' notebook or lapbook ☐ Define alloy and metal	☐ Add information about transition metals to the students' notebook or lapbook ☐ Complete the demonstration sheet ☐ {Work on the Periodic Table Weekly Review Sheet 4}

	5-Days-a-week Schedule				
	Day 1	**Day 2**	**Day 3**	**Day 4**	**Day 5**
Read	☐ Read "Transition Metals, Part 1"	☐ Read "Transition Metals, Part 2"	☐ {Work on memorizing the "Periodic Table" poem}	☐ Read "Transition Metals, Part 3"	☐ {Choose one or more of the additional resources to read from this week}
Do	☐ {Go on a Transition Metal Hunt}	☐ {Write an Iron Report}	☐ Do the Scientific Demonstration: Rusted	☐ {Do some Metal Plating}	☐ {Add the group to the Periodic Table Poster}
Write	☐ Add information about transition metals to the students' notebook or lapbook	☐ Add information about transition metals to the students' notebook or lapbook	☐ Complete the demonstration sheet ☐ Define alloy and metal	☐ Add information about transition metals to the students' notebook or lapbook	☐ {Work on the Periodic Table Weekly Review Sheet 4}

Read – Information Gathering

Reading Assignments
- ❑ *DK Eyewitness The Elements* pp. 22 23 "Transition Metals, Part 1"
  - ❓ What are some of the characteristics of transition metals?
- ❑ *DK Eyewitness The Elements* pp. 24-25 "Transition Metals, Part 2"
  - ❓ Can you describe some of the characteristics of iron?
- ❑ *DK Eyewitness The Elements* pp. 26-27 "Transition Metals, Part 3"
  - ❓ Can you describe some of the characteristics of copper?
  - ❓ Which transition metal was your favorite?

{Optional} Memory Work
- This week, continue to work on memorizing wthe *Periodic Table* poem. (SW p. 121)

{Optional} Additional Resources
Encyclopedias
- *DK Eyewitness The Elements* pp. 28-35 "Remaining Transition Metals"
- *Basher Science Complete Periodic Table* p. 34 "Transition Elements," p. 44 "Iron," p. 48 "Copper"
- *Scholastic's The Periodic Table* pp. 52-53 "Transition Metals," pp. 60-61 "Iron," pp.70-71 "Copper"
- *Usborne Science Encyclopedia* pp. 30-31 "Metals"

Library Books
- *The Transition Elements: The 37 Transition Metals (Understanding the Elements of the Periodic Table)* by Mary-Lane Kamberg
- *Iron (Elements)* by Giles Sparrow
- *Copper (The Elements)* by Richard Beatty

Do – Demonstration and Activities

Demonstration – Rusted
You will need the following:
- ✓ Steel wool
- ✓ Vinegar
- ✓ Jar with lid

Demonstration Instructions
1. Read the following introduction to the students.

   Last week, we learned about alkaline earth metals. This week, we are going to look at another group of metals, the transition metals. These elements make up the largest group on the periodic table. They are typically hard and shiny metals that are good conductors. In today's demonstration, we are going to see what happens to one of those transition metals when it is exposed to air.

2. Have the students place the steel wool in one of the jars and cover it with vinegar. Put the lid on the jar, and let the steel wool soak for two hours. (**Note –** This is done to remove any coating that may be on the steel wool so that the iron can react with the moist air.)
3. After two hours, have the students take the steel wool out and set it on a the jar lid. Let it sit undisturbed for 30 minutes.
4. After a half an hour has passed, observe the changes in the steel wool. As they are finishing their observations, ask the following questions:

    ? What happed to the steel wool?
5. Have the students draw what they see in the box on the demonstration sheet on SW p. 29 before you read the demonstration explanation to them.

Demonstration Explanation

The purpose of this demonstration was for the students to see what happens to iron, a transitional metal, in the air. When they are done, read the following to them:

> We saw the steel wool turn from a grey, metal color to a brownish-red color. This is because iron rusts, or oxidizes, when it is exposed to moist air. This is why iron we use in daily life is often coated with other metals or mixed with other elements to form rust-resistant alloys.

{Optional} Take the Demonstration Further

Have the students watch another redox reaction caused by air. You can do this by cutting an apple in half and letting it sit undisturbed for an hour. (*When you check it after an hour, the students should see that the slices are brownish. This is due to a redox reaction between the apple flesh and the oxygen in the air.*)

{Optional} Unit Project

✂ **Periodic Table Poster –** This week, have the students cut out the picture of the picture of the transition metals group, color it yellow, and add it to the blank table in the student workbook on p. 20 or on your wall-sized periodic table. The pictures for the groups of the periodic table are found in the SW Appendix on p. 129.

{Optional} Projects for This Week

✂ **Transition Metal Hunt –** Many of the elements in the transitional group are in items we have in our houses. Print out a copy of the transition metal hunt sheet from the Appendix on p. 193. Then, let the students hunt around the house for the metals listed on the sheet and color in any of the elements they find. If you want to make a game out of this, the person with the most elements colored in wins.

✂ **Iron Report –** Have the students research the uses of iron throughout history and write a one-paragraph report or create a poster advertisement with what they find.

✂ **Metal Plating** – Have the students turn an iron nail into one covered with copper. You will need white vinegar, salt, six pennies, a glass cup, and two iron nails. Have the students cover the bottom of the cup with a thin layer of salt. Then, add the pennies, and cover them with the vinegar. After 10 minutes, take the pennies out, and set them on a paper towel. Be sure to reserve the vinegar mixture. Add one of the nails to the vinegar solution, and leave the other one next to the glass. Let both of them sit undisturbed for 45 minutes. Take the nail out of the vinegar solution, and compare it to the nail that was left outside the glass. (*The students should see that the iron nail from the vinegar solution has a thin, shiny, brownish coating on it. The coating may or may not be completely covering the nail. After the pennies were removed, the vinegar solution contained copper ions. Over time, they adhered to the iron nail, giving it a thin, shiny, brownish coating of copper. This is a small glimpse of how metal (copper) plating works.*)

Write – Notebooking

Writing Assignments
- **Student Workbook** – Have the students dictate, copy, or write one to four sentences about transition metals on SW p. 28.
- **{Optional} Lapbooking Templates** – Have the students work on the Central Periodic Table. This week, have the students color the transition metals yellow.
- **{Optional} Lapbooking Templates** – Have the students work on the Transition Metals Tab-book on LT pp. 22-23. Have the students cut along the solid lines and color the group on the cover yellow. Next, have the students write several characteristics of transition metals on the characteristics tab, as well as several facts about iron and copper on the respective tabs. Then, have them line the pages up and staple the sheets together. Finally, glue the tab-book into the lapbook.
- **{Optional} Coloring Pages** – Have the students color the following pages: Transition Metals CP p. 17.

Vocabulary
Have the students look up and copy the definitions for the following words:
- **Alloy** – A mixture of two or more metals or a metal and a nonmetal. (SW p. 106)
- **Metal** – The largest class of elements; they are usually shiny and solid at room temperature. (SW p. 112)

{Optional} Weekly Review Sheet
- "Periodic Table Weekly Review Sheet 4" on SW p. 138.
    Answers:
    1. Good
    2. True
    3. Copper
    4. Answers will vary

Week 5: Boron Elements Lesson Plans

2-Days-a-week Schedule		
	Day 1	**Day 2**
Read	❑ Read "The Boron Group, Part 1" ❑ {Choose one or more of the additional resources to read from this week}	❑ Read "The Boron Group, Part 2" ❑ {Work on memorizing the "Periodic Table" poem}
Do	❑ {Make some Boron Slime or Add the group to the Periodic Table Poster}	❑ Do the Scientific Demonstration: Aluminum Gel
Write	❑ Add information about the boron elements to the students' notebook or lapbook ❑ Define metalloid	❑ Add information about the boron elements to the students' notebook or lapbook ❑ Complete the demonstration sheet ❑ {Work on the Periodic Table Weekly Review Sheet 5}

5-Days-a-week Schedule					
	Day 1	**Day 2**	**Day 3**	**Day 4**	**Day 5**
Read	❑ Read "The Boron Group, Part 1"	❑ {Work on memorizing the "Periodic Table" poem}	❑ Read "The Boron Group, Part 2"	❑ {Choose one or more of the additional resources to read from this week}	❑ {Choose one or more of the additional resources to read from this week}
Do	❑ {Watch the Aluminum Video}	❑ Do the Scientific Demonstration: Aluminum Gel	❑ {Make some Boron Slime}	❑ {Do the Indium Ink Research Project}	❑ {Add the group to the Periodic Table Poster}
Write	❑ Add information about the boron elements to the students' notebook or lapbook	❑ Complete the demonstration sheet	❑ Add information about the boron elements to the students' notebook or lapbook	❑ Define metalloid	❑ {Work on the Periodic Table Weekly Review Sheet 5}

Read – Information Gathering

Reading Assignments

- ❏ *DK Eyewitness The Elements* pp. 46-47 "The Boron Group, Part 1"
    - **?** What are some of the characteristics of boron group elements?
    - **?** Can you describe some of the characteristics of boron?
    - **?** Can you describe some of the characteristics of aluminum?
- ❏ *DK Eyewitness The Elements* pp. 48-49 "The Boron Group, Part 2"
    - **?** Can you describe some of the characteristics of galium?
    - **?** Which boron group element was your favorite?

{Optional} Memory Work
- This week, continue to work on memorizing the *Periodic Table* poem. (SW p. 121)

{Optional} Additional Resources

Encyclopedias
- *Basher Science Complete Periodic Table* p. 76 "Boron Elements," p. 78 "Boron," p. 80 "Aluminum"
- *Scholastic's The Periodic Table* pp. 102-103 "Poor Metals," p. 118 "Boron," pp. 104-105 "Aluminum"
- *Usborne Science Encyclopedia* p. 33 "Poor Metals"

Library Books
- *The Boron Elements: Boron, Aluminum, Gallium, Indium, Thallium (Understanding the Elements of the Periodic Table)* by Heather Hasan
- *Aluminum* by Heather Hasan
- *Boron (Elements)* by Richard Beatty

Do – Demonstration and Activities

Demonstration – Aluminum Gel

You will need the following:
- ✓ Alum powder
- ✓ Ammonia
- ✓ Clear jar
- ✓ Water

Demonstration Instructions

1. Read the following introduction to the students.

    Last week, we learned about transition metals. This week, we are going to look at elements in the boron group. These elements are not all similar. Boron is a metalloid: it has some of the properties of a metal, but not all of them. The rest of the elements in the group are metals. In today's demonstration, we are going to make a compound of aluminum.

2. Have the students add half cup of water to the jar.
3. Then, have them add a teaspoon of alum powder and stir until the powder dissolves.
4. Next, pour in a quarter cup of ammonia.
5. Allow the jar to sit undisturbed for about five minutes.
6. Finally, have the students draw what they see in the box on the demonstration sheet on SW p. 31 as you read the demonstration explanation to them.

Demonstration Explanation

The purpose of this demonstration was for the students to create an aluminum compound, which is one of the boron elements. When they are done, read the following to them:

> We saw the solution turn cloudy as soon as the ammonia is added. Then, after a few minutes, a white gel formed at the bottom of the jar. This gel is a compound of a main group metal, aluminum hydroxide. Once more, a chemical reaction created a new compound, and that new compound did not dissolve in water, so it precipitated or came out of the solution.

{Optional} Take the Demonstration Further

Have the students examine another aluminum-containing compound found in your kitchen, aluminum foil. Have them examine a sheet and note its appearance. If you want to learn about how foil is made, you can watch the following video:

- https://www.youtube.com/watch?v=0-gK6uom6aQ

{Optional} Unit Project

- **Periodic Table Poster** – This week, have the students cut out the picture of the boron elements group, color it light green, and add it to the blank table in the student workbook on p. 20 or on your wall-sized periodic table. The pictures for the groups of the periodic table are found in the SW Appendix on p. 129.

{Optional} Projects for This Week

- **Indium Ink Research** – Have the students learn about indium, which is used to make an electrically conductive ink. This ink is used in UPC codes, solar cells, and LCD screens. Older students can share what they have learned as a poster or in a paragraph.
- **Boron** – Have the students make slime using borax, a boron-containing compound. You will need gel glue, water, and Borax, which can be found in the laundry aisle. In a plastic baggie, have the students mix equal parts of glue and water. Meanwhile, in a cup, mix a quarter cup of water with half a teaspoon of Borax. Then, add the Borax solution to the baggie and have the students massage the bag for a few minutes until a nice firm slime has formed.
- **Aluminum** – Have the students watch a neat reaction where aluminum foil gets dissolved. The video can be viewed at the following link:

🖱 https://www.youtube.com/watch?v=AAKdc7PO3J0

Write – Notebooking

Writing Assignments
- ☐ **Student Workbook** – Have the students dictate, copy, or write one to four sentences about boron elements on SW p. 30.
- ☐ **{Optional} Lapbooking Templates** – Have the students work on the Central Periodic Table. This week, have the students color the boron elements light green.
- ☐ **{Optional} Lapbooking Templates** – Have the students work on the Boron Elements Flip-book on LT p. 24. Have the students cut along the solid lines and color the group on the cover light green. Next, have the students write several characteristics of boron elements on the characteristics tab as well as several facts about aluminum and boron on the respective tabs. Then, have them line the pages up and staple the sheets together. Finally, glue the flip-book into the lapbook.
- ☐ **{Optional} Coloring Pages** – Have the students color the following pages: Boron Elements CP p. 18.

Vocabulary
Have the students look up and copy the definitions for the following words:
- **Metalloid** – An element that shares some of the properties of metals and nonmetals. (SW p. 112)

{Optional} Weekly Review Sheet
- "Periodic Table Weekly Review Sheet 5" on SW p. 143.

    Answers:
    1. True
    2. False (*Galium has a much lower melting point than aluminum.*)
    3. An abundant
    4. Answers will vary

Week 6: Carbon Elements Lesson Plans

2-Days-a-week Schedule

	Day 1	Day 2
Read	☐ Read "The Carbon Group, Part 1" ☐ {Choose one or more of the additional resources to read from this week}	☐ Read "The Carbon Group, Part 2" ☐ {Work on memorizing the "Periodic Table" poem}
Do	☐ {Play with Silicone Putty or Add the group to the Periodic Table Poster}	☐ Do the Scientific Demonstration: Carbon Towers
Write	☐ Add information about the carbon elements to the students' notebook or lapbook ☐ Define nonmetal	☐ Add information about the carbon elements to the students' notebook or lapbook ☐ Complete the demonstration sheet ☐ {Work on the Periodic Table Weekly Review Sheet 6}

5-Days-a-week Schedule

	Day 1	Day 2	Day 3	Day 4	Day 5
Read	☐ Read "The Carbon Group, Part 1"	☐ {Work on memorizing the "Periodic Table" poem}	☐ Read "The Carbon Group, Part 2"	☐ {Choose one or more of the additional resources to read from this week}	☐ {Choose one or more of the additional resources to read from this week}
Do	☐ {Test for Carbon Rocks}	☐ Do the Scientific Demonstration: Carbon Towers	☐ {Make a Tin Can Luminary}	☐ {Play with Silicone Putty}	☐ {Add the group to the Periodic Table Poster}
Write	☐ Add information about the carbon elements to the students' notebook or lapbook	☐ Complete the demonstration sheet	☐ Add information about the carbon elements to the students' notebook or lapbook	☐ Define nonmetal	☐ {Work on the Periodic Table Weekly Review Sheet 6}

Read – Information Gathering

Reading Assignments

❑ *DK Eyewitness The Elements* pp. 50-51 "The Carbon Group, Part 1"
   ? What are some of the characteristics of carbon group elements?
   ? Can you describe some of the characteristics of carbon?

❑ *DK Eyewitness The Elements* pp. 52-53 "The Carbon Group, Part 2"
   ? Can you describe some of the characteristics of tin?
   ? Which carbon group element was your favorite?

{Optional} Memory Work

🔊 This week, continue to work on memorizing the *Periodic Table* poem. (SW p. 121)

{Optional} Additional Resources

Encyclopedias

📖 *Basher Science Complete Periodic Table* p. 86 "Carbon Elements," p. 88 "Carbon," p. 93 "Tin"

📖 *Scholastic's The Periodic Table* pp. 116-117 "Metalloids," pp. 162-163 "Carbon," p. 108 "Tin"

📖 *Usborne Science Encyclopedia* pp. 50-53 "Carbon"

Library Books

📖 *The Carbon Elements: Carbon, Silicon, Germanium, Tin, Lead (Understanding the Elements of the Periodic Table)* by Brian Belval

📖 *Carbon* by Linda Saucerman

📖 *Carbon (True Books: Elements)* by Salvatore Tocci

📖 *Tin (True Books: Elements)* by Salvatore Tocci

📖 *The Invention of the Silicon Chip: A Revolution in Daily Life* by Windsor Chorlton

Do – Demonstration and Activities

Demonstration – Carbon Towers

You will need the following:

- ✓ Sugar (3 Tbsp)
- ✓ Baking soda (1 tsp)
- ✓ Rubbing alcohol (2 Tbsp)
- ✓ Sand (1 cup)
- ✓ Aluminum pie pan
- ✓ Match

Demonstration Instructions

1. Read the following introduction to the students.

   Last week, we learned about the elements in the boron group. This week, we are going to learn about the elements in the carbon group. These elements are a mixture of nonmetals, such as carbon; metalloids, such as silicone; and metals, such as tin. In today's demonstration, we are going to make towers with carbon from a reaction.

Note – Do this experiment outdoors or in a well-ventilated place. Once, the fire goes out, wait for at least 10 minutes more before you throw the pie pan away.

2. Have the students pour the sand into the pie pan (or shallow dish). Then, have them form a well in the center of the sand pile.
3. As they do this, mix the sugar, baking soda, and rubbing alcohol in a cup. Then, spoon the paste into the sand well and light it with the match. Stand back and let the fire burn. Have the students observe what happens.
4. Read the demonstration explanation to the students and have them draw what they see on the demonstration sheet on SW p. 33.

Demonstration Explanation

The purpose of this demonstration was for the students to see a fun carbon reaction. When they are done, read the following to them:

> As the sugar mixture burned, towers of burned sugar form. This is a result of three chemical reactions that are all dependent on heat. The first of these reactions is combustion, which happens when sugar, which contains carbon, burns in the presence of oxygen. This produces carbon dioxide gas and water vapor. The gas from this reaction pushes up more of the sugar mixture. Meanwhile, some of the additional sugar mixture heats up, but because there is no oxygen, it doesn't burn up completely. This reaction produces solid carbon and more water vapor. This solid carbon gives the towers some shape along with the black color. Last, the baking soda also breaks down in the heat, producing solid sodium carbonate, carbon dioxide gas, and water vapor. The additional gases from this reaction help to give the towers their light, foamy texture.

{Optional} Take the Demonstration Further

Have the students use another reaction to produce carbon dioxide gas that can be used to put out a candle flame. The directions for this project can be found here:
- https://www.ronyestech.com/2020/05/how-to-make-carbon-dioxide-gas.html

{Optional} Unit Project

- **Periodic Table Poster –** This week, have the students cut out the picture of the carbon elements group, color it dark green, and add it to the blank table in the student workbook on p. 20 or on your wall-sized periodic table. The pictures for the groups of the periodic table are found in the SW Appendix on p. 129.

{Optional} Projects for This Week

- **Carbon Rocks –** Have the students test for the presence of carbon in rocks. Have them choose a rock, such as limestone, place it in a cup, and cover the rock with white vinegar. Have the students observe what happens. (*If bubbles are coming from the rock, it is carbonated.*)
- **Tin Can Luminary –** Have the students make a tin can luminary. You will need a tin can, a nail, a permanent marker, a hammer, and a candle. You can find the directions for this project from the following website:

🔗 http://www.thechaosandtheclutter.com/archives/tin-can-luminaries

✂ **Silicone Putty** – Have the students observe and play with the silicone polymer. You will need Silly Putty™ or other silicone polymer, a baggie, ice, a bowl, and hot water. Have the students pull the putty out slowly and quickly to see the differences in how the it reacts. Then, place the putty in the baggie and seal it. Fill the bowl with ice and nestle the baggie into the ice. Wait for five minutes. Have the students pull the putty out of the baggie and observe if it is cool to the touch. Have them quickly repeat the activities with the putty that were done before. (*How does the putty act differently after it has been in the ice?*) Next, place the putty back in the baggie, and seal it once more. Dump the ice out of the bowl and let it come to room temperature. After it does, fill the bowl halfway with hot water, and nestle the baggie into the water. You may need to weigh the baggie down with a glass or a rock. Wait for five minutes. Have the students pull the putty out of the baggie and observe if it is warm to the touch. Have them quickly repeat the activities with the putty that were done before. (*How does the putty act differently after it has been in the hot water?*)

Write – Notebooking

Writing Assignments

- ☐ **Student Workbook** – Have the students dictate, copy, or write one to four sentences about carbon elements on SW p. 32.
- ☐ **{Optional} Lapbooking Templates** – Have the students work on the Central Periodic Table. This week, have the students color the carbon elements dark green.
- ☐ **{Optional} Lapbooking Templates** – Have the students work on the Carbon Elements Flip-book on LT p. 25. Have the students cut along the solid lines and color the group on the cover dark green. Next, have the students write several characteristics of carbon elements on the characteristics tab as well as several facts about carbon and tin on the respective tabs. Then, line the pages up and staple the sheets together. Finally, glue the flip-book into the lapbook.
- ☐ **{Optional} Coloring Pages** – Have the students color the following page: Carbon Elements CP p. 19.

Vocabulary

Have the students look up and copy the definition for the following word:

- ✏ **Nonmetal** – A class of elements that can be nonshiny solids or gases. (SW p. 114)

{Optional} Weekly Review Sheet

- ♪ "Periodic Table Weekly Review Sheet 6" on SW p. 144.
    Answers:
    1. Metals, Nonmetals; 2. Students' answers will vary, but they should include that carbon is the basis for all life; 3. False (*Tin is often used in a metal alloy, including in bronze.*); 4. Answers will vary

Week 7: Nitrogen Elements Lesson Plans

2-Days-a-week Schedule		
	Day 1	**Day 2**
Read	❏ Read "The Nitrogen Group, Part 1" ❏ {Choose one or more of the additional resources to read from this week}	❏ Read "The Nitrogen Group, Part 2" ❏ {Work on memorizing the "Periodic Table" poem}
Do	❏ {Learn about the Nitrogen Cycle or Add the group to the Periodic Table Poster}	❏ Do the Scientific Demonstration: Shiny Pennies
Write	❏ Add information about the nitrogen elements to the students' notebook or lapbook ❏ Define essential element	❏ Add information about the nitrogen elements to the students' notebook or lapbook ❏ Complete the demonstration sheet ❏ {Work on the Periodic Table Weekly Review Sheet 7}

5-Days-a-week Schedule					
	Day 1	**Day 2**	**Day 3**	**Day 4**	**Day 5**
Read	❏ Read "The Nitrogen Group, Part 1"	❏ {Work on memorizing the "Periodic Table" poem}	❏ Read "The Nitrogen Group, Part 2"	❏ {Choose one or more of the additional resources to read from this week}	❏ {Choose one or more of the additional resources to read from this week}
Do	❏ {Learn about the Nitrogen Cycle}	❏ Do the Scientific Demonstration: Shiny Pennies	❏ {Compare the Types of Phosphorus}	❏ {Go on a Bismuth Hunt}	❏ {Add the group to the Periodic Table Poster}
Write	❏ Add information about the nitrogen elements to the students' notebook or lapbook	❏ Complete the demonstration sheet	❏ Add information about the nitrogen elements to the students' notebook or lapbook	❏ Define essential element	❏ {Work on the Periodic Table Weekly Review Sheet 7}

Read - Information Gathering

Reading Assignments

- ❑ *DK Eyewitness The Elements* pp. 54-55 "The Nitrogen Group, Part 1"
    - ❓ What are some of the characteristics of nitrogen group elements?
    - ❓ Can you describe some of the characteristics of nitrogen?

- ❑ *DK Eyewitness The Elements* pp. 56-57 "The Nitrogen Group, Part 2"
    - ❓ Can you describe some of the characteristics of arsenic?
    - ❓ Which nitrogen group element was your favorite?

{Optional} Memory Work
- 🗣 This week, continue to work on memorizing the *Periodic Table* poem. (SW p. 121)

{Optional} Additional Resources
Encyclopedias
- 📖 *Basher Science Complete Periodic Table* p. 96 "Nitrogen Elements," p. 98 "Nitrogen," p. 102 "Arsenic"
- 📖 *Scholastic's The Periodic Table* pp. 160-161 "Nonmetals," pp. 168-169 "Nitrogen," pp. 124-125 "Arsenic"

Library Books
- 📖 *The Nitrogen Elements (Understanding the Elements of the Periodic Table)* by Greg Roza
- 📖 *Nitrogen (True Books: Elements)* by Salvatore Tocci
- 📖 *Nitrogen* by Heather Hasan
- 📖 *Arsenic (Understanding the Elements of the Periodic Table)* by Greg Roza

Do - Demonstration and Activities

Demonstration - Shiny Pennies
You will need the following:
- ✓ Can of dark cola soda
- ✓ Glass
- ✓ Dirty pennies

Demonstration Instructions
1. Read the following introduction to the students.

    Last week, we learned about carbon elements. This week, we are looking at the elements in the nitrogen group. These elements in this group also contain nonmetals, metalloids, and metals. Nitrogen and phosphorus are two of the elements in this group that are elements essential for life. In today's demonstration, we are going to use one of these elements to clean a penny.

2. Have the students place several dirty pennies in a cup. Then, pour enough cola into the cup

to cover the pennies.
3. Set the cup aside and let it sit undisturbed overnight.
4. The next morning, fish out the pennies and have the students observe the differences. When you are done, pour the cola down the drain.
Note - Do not drink the cola as it now has copper ions in it!
5. Read the demonstration explanation to the students and have the students complete the demonstration sheet on SW p. 35.

Demonstration Explanation

The purpose of this demonstration was for the students to to see how phosphorus-containing liquid can help to clean a penny. When they are done, read the following to them:

> We saw that after a night in the cola our pennies were a lot cleaner. Dark cola has phosphoric acid in it, something that gives the soda its tangy flavor. This acid also breaks up the copper-oxygen compound that, with time, makes pennies dark and dull. That is how phosphorus, a nitrogen element, helps to clean up a penny.

{Optional} Take the Demonstration Further

Have the students see if they can get the same results from other kitchen acids, such as lemon juice, tea, milk, and other types of soda. (**Note-***The students will learn more about acids and bases in Unit 6.*)

{Optional} Unit Project

✂ **Periodic Table Poster –** This week, have the students cut out the picture of the nitrogen elements group, color it light blue, and add it to the blank table in the student workbook on p. 20 or on your wall-sized periodic table. The pictures for the groups of the periodic table are found in the SW Appendix on p. 129.

{Optional} Projects for This Week

✂ **Nitrogen Cycle –** Have the students learn more about the nitrogen cycle by watching the following video:
  https://www.youtube.com/watch?v=ZaFVfHftzpI
If you would like for your students to also learn about the phosphorus cycle, you can have them watch the following video:
  https://www.youtube.com/watch?v=wdAzQSuypCk

✂ **Types of Phosphorus –** Have the students learn about the three different types of phosphorus and their uses by reading *Usborne Science Encyclopedia* p. 55. You can also have older students create a chart with the similarities and differences of the three different types.

✂ **Bismuth Hunt –** Bismuth, one of the elements in the nitrogen elements group, is often used in makeup and medicine. Have the students head to your bathroom to look for items that contain bismuth. (*Look for things that have a pearly shine, because of bismuth oxychloride, and a certain pink antacid named for the element.*)

Write – Notebooking

Writing Assignments
- ☐ **Student Workbook** – Have the students dictate, copy, or write one to four sentences about nitrogen elements on SW p. 34.
- ☐ **{Optional} Lapbooking Templates** – Have the students work on the Central Periodic Table. This week, have the students color the nitrogen elements light blue.
- ☐ **{Optional} Lapbooking Templates** – Have the students work on the Nitrogen Elements Flip-book on LT p. 26. Have the students cut along the solid lines and color the group on the cover light blue. Next, have the students write several characteristics of nitrogen elements on the characteristics tab, as well as several facts about nitrogen and phosphorus on the respective tabs. Then, line the pages up and staple the sheets together. Finally, glue the flip-book into the lapbook.
- ☐ **{Optional} Coloring Pages** – Have the students color the following pages: Nitrogen Elements CP p. 20.

Vocabulary
Have the students look up and copy the definition for the following word:
- **Essential Element** – An element that is essential to life on earth, such as carbon, hydrogen, nitrogen, or oxygen. (SW p. 110)

{Optional} Weekly Review Sheet
- "Periodic Table Weekly Review Sheet 7" on SW p. 145.

    Answers:
    1. True
    2. 80 %
    3. True
    4. Answers will vary

Week 8: Oxygen Elements Lesson Plans

2-Days-a-week Schedule		
	Day 1	**Day 2**
Read	☐ Read "The Oxygen Group, Part 1" ☐ {Choose one or more of the additional resources to read from this week}	☐ Read "The Oxygen Group, Part 2" ☐ {Work on memorizing the "Periodic Table" poem}
Do	☐ {Do the Smelly Sulfur activity or Add the group to the Periodic Table Poster}	☐ Do the Scientific Demonstration: Breathing Flame
Write	☐ Add information about oxygen elements to the students' notebook or lapbook ☐ Define oxidation	☐ Add information about oxygen elements to the students' notebook or lapbook ☐ Complete the demonstration sheet ☐ {Work on the Periodic Table Weekly Review Sheet 8}

5-Days-a-week Schedule					
	Day 1	**Day 2**	**Day 3**	**Day 4**	**Day 5**
Read	☐ Read "The Oxygen Group, Part 1"	☐ Read "The Oxygen Group, Part 2"	☐ {Work on memorizing the "Periodic Table" poem}	☐ {Choose one or more of the additional resources to read from this week}	☐ {Choose one or more of the additional resources to read from this week}
Do	☐ {Watch the Oxygen Video}	☐ {Do the Smelly Sulfur activity}	☐ Do the Scientific Demonstration: Breathing Flame	☐ {Research Selenium}	☐ {Add the group to the Periodic Table Poster}
Write	☐ Add information about oxygen elements to the students' notebook or lapbook	☐ Add information about oxygen elements to the students' notebook or lapbook	☐ Complete the demonstration sheet	☐ Define oxidation	☐ {Work on the Periodic Table Weekly Review Sheet 8}

Read – Information Gathering

Reading Assignments

- ❑ *DK Eyewitness The Elements* pp. 58-59 "The Oxygen Group, Part 1"
  - ❓ What are some of the characteristics of oxygen group elements?
  - ❓ Can you describe some of the characteristics of oxygen?
- ❑ *DK Eyewitness The Elements* pp. 60-61 "The Oxygen Group, Part 2"
  - ❓ Can you describe some of the characteristics of sulfur?
  - ❓ Which oxygen group element was your favorite?

{Optional} Memory Work

- This week, continue to work on memorizing the *Periodic Table* poem. (SW p. 121)

{Optional} Additional Resources

Encyclopedias

- *Basher Science Complete Periodic Table* p. 106 "Oxygen Elements," p. 108 "Oxygen," p. 110 "Sulfur"
- *Scholastic's The Periodic Table* pp. 158-159 "Life in Color" (Omit sections on the halogens and noble gases), pp. 174-175 "Oxygen," p. 176 "Sulfur"
- *Usborne Science Encyclopedia* pp. 92-93 "Organic Chemistry"

Library Books

- *The Oxygen Elements: Oxygen, Sulfur, Selenium, Tellurium, Polonium (Understanding the Elements of the Periodic Table)* by Laura La Bella
- *Nonmetals (Material Matters/Freestyle Express)* by Carol Baldwin
- *Oxygen (True Books: Elements)* by Salvatore Tocci
- *Sulfur (The Elements)* by Richard Beatty

Do – Demonstration and Activities

Demonstration Breathing Flame

You will need the following:
- ✓ Candle
- ✓ Match
- ✓ Glass jar

Demonstration Instructions

1. Read the following introduction to the students.

   Last week, we learned about nitrogen elements. This week, we are learning about the oxygen elements. Again, these elements are a mixture of nonmetals, metalloids, and metals. But the group is named after a very important element— oxygen. This element helps to keep us alive and helps a fire to keep burning. In

today's demonstration, we will see what happens to a flame when we remove the oxygen.
2. (**Adults Only**) Use the match to light the candle.
3. Have the students observe the flame.
4. (**Adults Only**) Then, turn the jar upside down, and place it over the candle.
5. Have the students observe what happens and draw it on the demonstration sheet on SW p. 37 as you read the demonstration explanation to them.

Demonstration Explanation

The purpose of this demonstration was for the students to see how oxygen is necessary for a flame to burn. When they are done, read the following to them:

> When the candle was uncovered, the flame burned. However once we covered the candle with the jar, we saw the flame burn for a bit and then go out. This is because the oxygen that is trapped inside the jar is used up by the flame. Once it is gone, the flame goes out. A candle wick burns through a reaction called combustion. For this to occur, oxygen needs to be present in the air around the candle.

{Optional} Take the Demonstration Further

Repeat the demonstration, only this time remove the jar covering the candle just before the flame goes out. What happens this time? (*The flame should burn strongly once more.*)

{Optional} Unit Project

✂ **Periodic Table Poster** – This week, have the students cut out the picture of the oxygen elements group, color it dark blue, and add it to the blank table in the student workbook on p. 20 or on your wall-sized periodic table. The pictures for the groups of the periodic table are found in the SW Appendix on p. 129.

{Optional} Projects for This Week

✂ **Oxygen Video** – Have the students watch the following video about oxygen:
  http://easyscienceforkids.com/oxygen-element-video-for-kids/

✂ **Smelly Sulfur** – Have the students experience the smell of sulfur! You will need a vegetable with a high sulfur content, such as cabbage, brussel sprouts, or turnips. Cut the vegetable in half, smell both halves, and set one half aside. Then, cut the remaining half in half again and boil the two quarters. After 10 minutes remove one of the quarters and have the students compare the smells between the cooked and uncooked portions. Wait 10 more minutes and then remove the remaining quarter from the boiling water. Have the students compare the smells of all three slices. (*The students should note an increasing "rotten-eggs" smell in the cooked portions of the vegetable. The heat causes the bonds to break, which releases the stinky sulfur-containing compound, hydrogen sulfide.*)

✂ **Selenium Research** – Have the students research a bit about selenium and its uses.

Selenium is one of the most abundant oxygen elements on earth after oxygen. Older students can share what they have learned as a poster or in a paragraph.

Write – Notebooking

Writing Assignments
- **Student Workbook** – Have the students dictate, copy, or write one to four sentences about the oxygen elements on SW p. 36.
- **{Optional} Lapbooking Templates** – Have the students work on the Central Periodic Table. This week, have the students color the oxygen elements dark blue.
- **{Optional} Lapbooking Templates** – Have the students work on the Oxygen Elements Flip-book on LT p. 27. Have the students cut along the solid lines and color the group on the cover dark blue. Next, have the students write several characteristics of oxygen elements on the characteristics tab, as well as several facts about oxygen and sulfur on the respective tabs. Then, line the pages up and staple the sheets together. Finally, glue the flip-book into the lapbook.
- **{Optional} Coloring Pages** – Have the students color the following pages: Oxygen Elements CP p. 21.

Vocabulary
Have the students look up and copy the definition for the following word:
- **Oxidation** – A chemical reaction in which a substance combines with oxygen. (SW p. 114)

{Optional} Weekly Review Sheet
- "Periodic Table Weekly Review Sheet 8" on SW p. 146.
    Answers:
    1. Important
    2. Students' answers will vary, but they should include that oxygen is fuel for our body or that it is the powerhouse behind most chemical reactions on Earth.
    3. True
    4. Answers will vary

Week 9: Halogens Lesson Plans

2-Days-a-week Schedule		
	Day 1	**Day 2**
Read	❑ Read "Halogens, Part 1" ❑ {Choose one or more of the additional resources to read from this week}	❑ Read "Halogens, Part 2" ❑ {Work on memorizing the "Periodic Table" poem}
Do	❑ {Make a Fluoride Egg or Add the group to the Periodic Table Poster}	❑ Do the Scientific Demonstration: Iodine Testing
Write	❑ Add information about halogens to the students' notebook or lapbook ❑ Define ion	❑ Add information about halogens to the students' notebook or lapbook ❑ Complete the demonstration sheet ❑ {Work on the Periodic Table Weekly Review Sheet 9}

5-Days-a-week Schedule					
	Day 1	**Day 2**	**Day 3**	**Day 4**	**Day 5**
Read	❑ Read "Halogens, Part 1"	❑ Read "Halogens, Part 2"	❑ {Work on memorizing the "Periodic Table" poem}	❑ {Choose one or more of the additional resources to read from this week}	❑ {Choose one or more of the additional resources to read from this week}
Do	❑ {Make a Fluoride Egg}	❑ {Write a Secret Message}	❑ Do the Scientific Demonstration: Iodine Testing	❑ {Watch the Halogen Video}	❑ {Add the group to the Periodic Table Poster}
Write	❑ Add information about halogens to the students' notebook or lapbook	❑ Add information about halogens to the students' notebook or lapbook	❑ Complete the demonstration sheet	❑ Define ion	❑ {Work on the Periodic Table Weekly Review Sheet 9}

Read – Information Gathering

Reading Assignments

❑ *DK Eyewitness The Elements* pp. 62-63 "Halogens, Part 1"
  ? What are some of the characteristics of halogen elements?
  ? Can you describe some of the characteristics of fluorine?

❑ *DK Eyewitness The Elements* pp. 64-65 "Halogens, Part 2"
  ? Can you describe some of the characteristics of iodine?
  ? Which halogen element was your favorite?

{Optional} Memory Work

🕮 This week, continue to work on memorizing the *Periodic Table* poem. (SW p. 121)

{Optional} Additional Resources

Encyclopedias
📖 *Basher Science Complete Periodic Table* p. 116 "Halogens," p. 118 "Fluorine," p. 124 "Iodine"
📖 *Scholastic's The Periodic Table* pp. 182-183 "Halogens," p. 184 "Fluorine," p. 189 "Iodine"
📖 *Usborne Science Encyclopedia* pp. 48-49 "Halogens"

Library Books
📖 *Fluorine (Understanding the Elements of the Periodic Table)* by Heather Hasan
📖 *The Elements: Iodine* by Leon Gray
📖 *Iodine (Understanding the Elements of the Periodic Table)* by Kristi Lew

Do – Demonstration and Activities

Demonstration – Iodine Testing

You will need the following:
- ✓ Small piece of potato
- ✓ Small piece of bread
- ✓ Small piece of fruit
- ✓ Iodine swab

Demonstration Instructions

1. Read the following introduction to the students.

   Last week, we learned about the elements in the oxygen group. This week, we are moving onto the halogens. These elements react quickly with metals to form salts. In today's demonstration, we are going to use this quick reaction to test for the presence of a starch.

2. Have students swab the potato sample with the iodine swab and watch what happens. Have the students write their observations on the chart on the demonstration sheet on SW p. 39.

3. Have the students repeat the process with the bread.

4. Have the students repeat the process with the fruit.
5. Then, read the demonstration explanation to the students and have the students finish the demonstration sheet.

Demonstration Explanation

The purpose of this demonstration was for the students to see how iodine, a halogen, can help identify the presence of a starch. When they are done, read the following to them:

> We saw the color of the iodine change when it touched the bread and potato, but it stayed the same when it touched the fruit. Iodine changes from brown-black to blue-purple in the presence of a starch. Both bread and potatoes have starch in them, which is why we saw the iodine change color when it touched those samples. Fruit does not typically contain starch, so the iodine remains brown-black when it touches that sample.

{Optional} Take the Demonstration Further

Have the students test other foods they choose for the presence of starch.

{Optional} Unit Project

✂ **Periodic Table Poster** – This week, have the students cut out the picture of the halogens group, color it purple, and add it to the blank table in the student workbook on p. 20 or on your wall-sized periodic table. The pictures for the groups of the periodic table are found in the SW Appendix on p. 131.

{Optional} Projects for This Week

✂ **Halogen Video** – Have the students watch the following video showing the different reactivities of the halogens:
   https://www.youtube.com/watch?v=saLvwX3_p1s

✂ **Fluoride Egg** – Fluorine is often used in toothpaste to help protect the enamel on teeth from being dissolved. Have the students test this ability using an egg. You will need two eggs, fluoride toothpaste, plastic wrap, white vinegar, and an egg. Coat one of the eggs with the toothpaste, wrap it in plastic wrap, and set it in the fridge overnight. After 24 hours, gently rinse off any excess toothpaste with warm water and mark it with an "F" using a permanent maker. Then, set both eggs in a cup, cover them with vinegar, and watch what happens. (*The students should see that the egg marked with an "F" does not dissolve nearly as quickly as the one without.*)

✂ **Secret Message** – Have the students use iodine to reveal a secret message. You will need a shallow pan, tincture of iodine, water, paper, Q-tip, lemon juice, and a cup. Pour some lemon juice into a cup. Then, have the students use the lemon juice and Q-tip to write a message on the paper. Meanwhile, mix together a cup of water and 20 drops of tincture of iodine in the bowl until well mixed. Once the juice has dried on the paper, have the students give you the sheet. Place it into the iodine solution in the pan to reveal the message!

Write – Notebooking

Writing Assignments
- ☐ **Student Workbook** – Have the students dictate, copy, or write one to four sentences about halogens on SW p. 38.
- ☐ **{Optional} Lapbooking Templates** – Have the students work on the Central Periodic Table. This week, have the students color the halogens purple.
- ☐ **{Optional} Lapbooking Templates** – Have the students work on the Halogens Flip-book on LT p. 28. Have the students cut along the solid lines and color the group on the cover purple. Next, have the students write several characteristics of halogens on the characteristics tab, as well as several facts about fluorine and iodine on the respective tabs. Then, have them line the pages up and staple the sheets together. Finally, glue the flip-book into the lapbook.
- ☐ **{Optional} Coloring Pages** – Have the students color the following pages: Halogens CP p. 22.

Vocabulary
Have the students look up and copy the definition for the following word:
- **Ion** – An atom or group of atoms that has become charged by gaining or losing one or more electrons. (SW p. 112)

{Optional} Weekly Review Sheet
- "Periodic Table Weekly Review Sheet 9" on SW p. 147.

    Answers:
    1. False (*Fluorine is the most reactive element in the halogen group.*)
    2. Salt-forming, salts
    3. True
    4. Answers will vary

Week 10: Noble Gases Lesson Plans

2-Days-a-week Schedule

	Day 1	Day 2
Read	❏ Read "Noble Gases, Part 1" ❏ {Choose one or more of the additional resources to read from this week}	❏ Read "Noble Gases, Part 2" ❏ {Work on memorizing the "Periodic Table" poem}
Do	❏ {Learn about Dangerous Noble Gases or Add the group to the Periodic Table Poster}	❏ Do the Scientific Demonstration: Funny Voice
Write	❏ Add information about noble gases to the students' notebook or lapbook ❏ Define inert	❏ Add information about noble gases to the students' notebook or lapbook ❏ Complete the demonstration sheet ❏ {Work on the Periodic Table Weekly Review Sheet 10}

5-Days-a-week Schedule

	Day 1	Day 2	Day 3	Day 4	Day 5
Read	❏ Read "Noble Gases, Part 1"	❏ Read "Noble Gases, Part 2"	❏ {Work on memorizing the "Periodic Table" poem}	❏ {Choose one or more of the additional resources to read from this week}	❏ {Choose one or more of the additional resources to read from this week}
Do	❏ {Go look for Neon Lights}	❏ {Learn about Dangerous Noble Gases}	❏ Do the Scientific Demonstration: Funny Voice		❏ {Add the group to the Periodic Table Poster}
Write	❏ Add information about noble gases to the students' notebook or lapbook	❏ Add information about noble gases to the students' notebook or lapbook	❏ Complete the demonstration sheet	❏ Define inert	❏ {Work on the Periodic Table Weekly Review Sheet 10}

Read – Information Gathering

Reading Assignments

❑ *DK Eyewitness The Elements* pp. 66-67 "Noble Gases, Part 1"
  ? What are some of the characteristics of noble gases elements?
  ? Can you describe some of the characteristics of helium?

❑ *DK Eyewitness The Elements* pp. 68-69 "Noble Gases, Part 2"
  ? Can you describe some of the characteristics of krypton?
  ? Which noble gases was your favorite?

{Optional} Memory Work

✊ This week, continue to work on memorizing the *Periodic Table* poem. (SW p. 121)

{Optional} Additional Resources

Encyclopedias

📖 *Basher Science Complete Periodic Table* p. 128 "Noble Gases," p. 192 "Helium," p. 193 "Neon"
📖 *Scholastic's The Periodic Table* pp. 190-191 "Noble Gases," p. 192 "Helium"
📖 *Usborne Science Encyclopedia* p. 63 "Noble Gases Section"

Library Books

📖 *Hydrogen and the Noble Gases (True Books: Elements)* by Salvatore Tocci
📖 *Hooray for Helium!: Understanding the 2nd Most Common Element (The Chem Kids)* by Blake Washington and Mallette Pagano
📖 *Krypton (Understanding the Elements of the Periodic Table)* by Janey Levy

Do – Demonstration and Activities

Demonstration – Funny Voice

You will need the following:
- ✓ Helium-filled balloon
- ✓ Scissors

Demonstration Instructions

1. Read the following introduction to the students.

    Last week, we learned about the halogens, one of the most reactive groups of elements. This week, we are going to learn about noble gases, one of the least reactive groups of elements. Helium is the first element in the group. In today's demonstration, we are going to see what helium does to our voices.

2. Pinch the base of a helium-filled balloon just under the knot and cut off the end so that you can get some of the gas to release.

3. Exhale completely and place the cut balloon just under your chin. (**CAUTION** – *Helium is*

nontoxic, but it can cause lightheadedness. Do NOT let the students do this activity – you need to demonstrate it for them. Do NOT repeat it more than once, and be sure to follow the directions.)

4. As you inhale, open the balloon so that you breathe in some of the helium. Then, start to talk or sing so that the students can observe the difference in your voice.
5. Read the demonstration explanation to the students and have the students complete the demonstration sheet on SW p. 41.

Demonstration Explanation

The purpose of this demonstration was for the students to see how helium can change the sound of your voice. When they are done, read the following to them:

> With a bit of helium, our voices had a squeaky quality to them and they were a bit higher. This is because helium is six times lighter than air, so the sound waves of our voices speed up as they pass through the gas, causing our voices to sound squeaky.

{Optional} Take the Demonstration Further

Have the students learn more about the history of helium-filled blimps by watching the following video:
- https://www.youtube.com/watch?v=vfpv6JXMaGM

{Optional} Unit Project

- **Periodic Table Poster** – This week, have the students cut out the picture of the noble gases group, color it gray, and add it to the blank table in the student workbook on p. 20 or on your wall-sized periodic table. The pictures for the groups of the periodic table are found in the SW Appendix on p. 131.

{Optional} Projects for This Week

- **Dangerous Noble Gases** – Radon is a noble gas that is one of the products of radioactive decay. It can build up in the basements of homes that sit over natural deposits of thorium or uranium. If there is radon present in a house, contractors can install a system that flushes it out. See if you live in a radon zone:
  - http://www.epa.gov/radon/epa-map-radon-zones
- **Neon** – Head out on a field trip to look for neon lights! You may want to read the following article beforehand so that you understand how neon lights work and what elements give them their color:
  - http://www.ehow.com/how-does_4927221_neon-its-colors.html

Write – Notebooking

Writing Assignments

- [ ] **Student Workbook** – Have the students dictate, copy, or write one to four sentences about noble gases on SW p. 40.

- ☐ **{Optional} Lapbooking Templates –** Have the students work on the Central Periodic Table. This week, have the students color the noble gases gray.
- ☐ **{Optional} Lapbooking Templates –** Have the students work on the Noble Gases Flip-book on LT p. 29. Have the students cut along the solid lines and color the group on the cover gray. Next, have the students write several characteristics of noble gases on the characteristics tab as well as several facts about helium and neon on the respective tabs. Then, line the pages up and staple the sheets together. Finally, glue the flip-book into the lapbook.
- ☐ **{Optional} Coloring Pages –** Have the students color the following pages: Noble Gases CP p. 23.

Vocabulary

Have the students look up and copy the definitions for the following words:
- **Inert –** An element that is completely nonreactive. (SW p. 111)

{Optional} Weekly Review Sheet

- "Periodic Table Weekly Review Sheet 10" on SW p. 148.
    Answers:
    1. Least
    2. False (*Helium is lighter than air.*)
    3. Lights
    4. Answers will vary

Week 11: Lanthanides Lesson Plans

2-Days-a-week Schedule		
	Day 1	**Day 2**
Read	❑ Read "Lanthanides, Part 1" ❑ {Choose one or more of the additional resources to read from this week}	❑ Read "Lanthanides, Part 2" ❑ {Work on memorizing the "Periodic Table" poem}
Do	❑ {Play with Neodymium Magnets or Add the group to the Periodic Table Poster}	❑ Do the Scientific Demonstration: Moving Pencils
Write	❑ Add information about lanthanides to the students' notebook or lapbook ❑ Define refraction	❑ Add information about lanthanides to the students' notebook or lapbook ❑ Complete the demonstration sheet ❑ {Work on the Periodic Table Weekly Review Sheet 11}

5-Days-a-week Schedule					
	Day 1	**Day 2**	**Day 3**	**Day 4**	**Day 5**
Read	❑ Read "Lanthanides, Part 1"	❑ Read "Lanthanides, Part 2"	❑ {Work on memorizing the "Periodic Table" poem}	❑ {Choose one or more of the additional resources to read from this week}	❑ {Choose one or more of the additional resources to read from this week}
Do	❑ {Play with Refraction Prisms}	❑ {Play with Neodymium Magnets}	❑ Do the Scientific Demonstration: Moving Pencils	❑ {Do the Terbium Rub activity}	❑ {Add the group to the Periodic Table Poster}
Write	❑ Add information about lanthanides to the students' notebook or lapbook	❑ Add information about lanthanides to the students' notebook or lapbook	❑ Complete the demonstration sheet	❑ Define refraction	❑ {Work on the Periodic Table Weekly Review Sheet 11}

Read – Information Gathering

Reading Assignments

❑ *DK Eyewitness The Elements* pp. 36-37 "Lanthanides, Part 1"
  ❓ What are some of the characteristics of lanthanide elements?
  ❓ Can you describe some of the characteristics of lanthanum?

❑ *DK Eyewitness The Elements* pp. 38-39 "Lanthanides, Part 2"
  ❓ Can you describe some of the characteristics of ytterbium?
  ❓ Which lanthanide element was your favorite?

{Optional} Memory Work

🗣 This week, continue to work on memorizing the *Periodic Table* poem. (SW p. 121)

{Optional} Additional Resources

Encyclopedias

📖 *Basher Science Complete Periodic Table* p. 140 "Lanthanides," p. 142 "Lanthanum," p. 156 "Ytterbium"

📖 *Scholastic's The Periodic Table* pp. 128-129 "Lanthanoids," p. 130 "Lanthanum," p. 138 "Ytterbium"

Library Books

📖 *The Lanthanides (Elements)* by Richard Beatty

Do – Demonstration and Activities

Demonstration – Moving Pencils

You will need the following:
- ✓ 3 Cups
- ✓ 3 Pencils
- ✓ 3 Clear liquids (i.e., water, alcohol, and corn syrup)

Demonstration Instructions

1. Read the following introduction to the students.

   Last week, we learned about noble gases. This week, we are moving onto the lanthanide elements. These elements are known as the rare earth elements, even though they are not super rare, just difficult to isolate. In today's demonstration, we are going to see one thing that a lanthanide can be used to do.

2. Fill each of the three cups halfway with one of the clear liquids.
3. Have the students place a pencil in each of the cups.
4. Then, have them observe what has happened to the pencils.
5. Read the demonstration explanation to the students and have the students complete the demonstration sheet on SW p. 43.

Demonstration Explanation

The purpose of this demonstration was for the students to understand the concept of refraction. When they are done, read the following to them:

> We saw that the pencils appeared to break and shift or move in the different liquids. This is due to refraction, or the bending of light. One of the lanthanide elements, lanthanum, is often used in quality glass lenses so that the image we see is closer to the original one.

{Optional} Take the Demonstration Further

Have the students repeat the demonstration with other clear liquids, such as baby oil.

{Optional} Unit Project

- **Periodic Table Poster** – This week, have the students cut out the picture of the lanthanides group, color it brown, and add it to the blank table in the student workbook on p. 20 or on your wall-sized periodic table. The pictures for the groups of the periodic table are found in the SW Appendix on p. 131.

{Optional} Projects for This Week

- **Refraction Prism** – Have the students play with a prism, which refracts, or bends, the different wavelengths of light at different angles to create a rainbow.
- **Neodymium Magnets** – Have the students play with neodymium magnets! Be careful to supervise them well with this activity as neodymium magnets are very strong and very dangerous if swallowed.
- **Terbium Rub** – Have the students excite some electrons to make a bulb glow without plugging it in. You will need a woolen mitten or glove and a fluorescent bulb. Head into a dark room, rub the bulb with the woolen mitten, and watch what happens! (*Elements like terbium, a lanthanide that is sometimes used to coat fluorescent bulbs, glow when they are hit by a beam of electrons. When you rub the bulb, you create static electricity, which is basically excited electrons!*)

Write – Notebooking

Writing Assignments

- ☐ **Student Workbook** – Have the students dictate, copy, or write one to four sentences about lanthanides on SW p. 42.
- ☐ **{Optional} Lapbooking Templates** – Have the students work on the Central Periodic Table. This week, have the students color the lanthanides brown.
- ☐ **{Optional} Lapbooking Templates** – Have the students work on the Lanthanides Flip-book on LT p. 30. Have the students cut along the solid lines and color the group on the cover brown. Next, have the students write several characteristics of lanthanides on the characteristics tabs, as well as several facts about lanthanum and neodymium on the

respective tabs. Then, line the pages up and staple the sheets together. Finally, glue the flipbook into the lapbook.

- ☐ **{Optional} Coloring Pages** – Have the students color the following pages: Lanthanides CP p. 24.

Vocabulary

Have the students look up and copy the definition for the following word:

- **Refraction** – The bending of light as it passes through a different medium. (SW p. 116)

{Optional} Weekly Review Sheet

- "Periodic Table Weekly Review Sheet 11" on SW p. 149.
    - Answers:
    1. True
    2. Steel, Good lens
    3. Very
    4. Answers will vary

Week 12: Actinides Lesson Plans

2-Days-a-week Schedule		
	Day 1	Day 2
Read	❏ Read "Actinides, Part 1 & 2" ❏ {Choose one or more of the additional resources to read from this week}	❏ Read "Actinides, Part 3" ❏ {Work on memorizing the "Periodic Table" poem}
Do	❏ {Watch a video about Uranium Power or Add the group to the Periodic Table Poster}	❏ Do the Scientific Demonstration: Half-life
Write	❏ Add information about actinides to the students' notebook or lapbook ❏ Define radioactive decay	❏ Add information about actinides to the students' notebook or lapbook ❏ Complete the demonstration sheet ❏ {Work on the Periodic Table Weekly Review Sheet 12}

5-Days-a-week Schedule					
	Day 1	Day 2	Day 3	Day 4	Day 5
Read	❏ Read "Actinides, Part 1"	❏ Read "Actinides, Part 2"	❏ {Work on memorizing the "Periodic Table" poem}	❏ Read "Actinides, Part 3"	❏ {Choose one or more of the additional resources to read from this week}
Do	❏ {Learn about Americium Detectors}	❏ {Watch a video about Uranium Power}	❏ Do the Scientific Demonstration: Half-life	❏ {Add the group to the Periodic Table Poster}	❏ {Review what the students have learend about the periodic table}
Write	❏ Add information about actinides to the students' notebook or lapbook	❏ Add information about actinides to the students' notebook or lapbook	❏ Complete the demonstration sheet ❏ Define radioactive decay	❏ Add information about actinides to the students' notebook or lapbook	❏ {Work on the Periodic Table Weekly Review Sheet 12}

Read – Information Gathering

Reading Assignments

- ❑ *DK Eyewitness The Elements* pp. 40-41 "Actinides, Part 1"
    - **?** What are some of the characteristics of actinides?
    - **?** Can you describe some of the characteristics of americium?
- ❑ *DK Eyewitness The Elements* pp. 42-43 "Actinides, Part 2"
    - **?** Can you describe some of the characteristics of uranium?
    - **?** Can you describe some of the characteristics of plutonium?
- ❑ *DK Eyewitness The Elements* pp. 44-45 "Actinides, Part 3"
    - **?** Which actinide element was your favorite?

{Optional} Memory Work

- This week, continue to work on memorizing the *Periodic Table* poem. (SW p. 121)

{Optional} Additional Resources

Encyclopedias

- *Basher Science Complete Periodic Table* p. 158 "Actinides," p. 163 "Uranium," p. 167 "Americium"
- *Scholastic's The Periodic Table* pp. 140-141 "Actinoids," pp. 144-145 "Uranium," p. 154 "Americium"

Library Books

- *Radioactive Elements* by Tom Jackson
- *The 15 Lanthanides and the 15 Actinides (Understanding the Elements of the Periodic Table)* by Kristi Lew

Do – Demonstration and Activities

Demonstration – Half-life

You will need the following:
- ✓ Bite-sized food, such as raisins or cereal puffs
- ✓ Timer

Demonstration Instructions

1. Read the following introduction to the students.

    Last week, we learned about lanthanides. This week, we are learning about acitinides. These elements are a very radioactive bunch. Radioactive elements decay over time in a set amount of time called a half-life. In today's demonstration, we are going to use food to see what a half-life looks like.

2. Give the students 32 pieces of the bite-sized food.
3. After two minutes, have them eat 16 pieces.

4. After two more minutes, have them eat eight pieces.
5. After two more minutes, have them eat four pieces.
6. After two more minutes, have them eat two pieces.
7. After two more minutes, have them eat one piece.
8. After two more minutes, have them break the one piece in half and eat one of the halves.
9. After two more minutes, have the students eat any of the remaining crumbs.
10. Read the demonstration explanation to the students and have the students complete the demonstration sheet on SW p. 45.

Demonstration Explanation

The purpose of this demonstration was for the students to understand what a half-life is. When they are done, read the following to them:

> This demonstration gives us a mental picture of how a half-life works. Many of the actinide elements are radioactive, which means that they are unstable so the elements decay with a half-life. The half-life period depends on the element and how radioactive it is.

{Optional} Unit Project

✂ **Periodic Table Poster** – This week, have the students cut out the picture of the actinides group, color it white, and add it to the blank table in the student workbook on p. 20 or on your wall-sized periodic table. The pictures for the groups of the periodic table are found in the SW Appendix on p. 131.

{Optional} Projects for This Week

✂ **Americium Detectors** – Have the students learn about how smoke detectors, which contain americium, work. You will need a working smoke detector, a hair dryer, and a bottle of baby powder. Have the students turn the hair dryer on high, aim it at the smoke detector, count to five, and then turn the dryer off. (*The students should see that the heat from the dryer did not set off the alarm.*) Then, hold the detector above the bottle of baby power and squeeze the bottle gently to create a few puffs of baby powder. (*This time the students should see that the smoke detector went off. This is because the americium in the smoke detector charges the nearby air and when new molecules float through this zone, it changes the charge and causes the alarm to sound.*)

✂ **Uranium Power** – Have the students learn more about nuclear power by watching the following video:
   🖱 https://www.youtube.com/watch?v=d7LO8lL4Ai4
   Note–*This video does touch on the dangers of nuclear power vs. other power methods. Please preview this video to make sure it is appropriate for your child.*

✂ **Review** – Have the students review what they have learned so far about the periodic table.

Write – Notebooking

Writing Assignments
- ☐ **Student Workbook** – Have the students dictate, copy, or write one to four sentences about actinides on SW p. 44.
- ☐ **{Optional} Lapbooking Templates** – Have the students work on the Central Periodic Table. This week, have the students color the actinides white.
- ☐ **{Optional} Lapbooking Templates** – Have the students work on the Actinides Flip-book on LT p. 31. Have the students cut along the solid lines and color the group on the cover white. Next, have the students write several characteristics of actinides on the characteristics tabs, as well as several facts about uranium and americium on the respective tab. Then, line the pages up and staple the sheets together. Finally, glue the flip-book into the lapbook.
- ☐ **{Optional} Lapbooking Templates** – Have the students finish their lapbook. Have them cut out and color the poem on LT p. 32. Once they are done, have them glue the sheet into their lapbook.
- ☐ **{Optional} Coloring Pages** – Have the students color the following pages: Actinides CP p. 25.

Vocabulary
Have the students look up and copy the definition for the following word:
- **Radioactive Decay** – The process by which a nucleus ejects particles through radiation become the nucleus of a series of different elements until stability is reached. (SW p. 116)

{Optional} Weekly Review Sheet
- "Periodic Table Weekly Review Sheet 12" on SW p. 150.
    Answers:
    1. True
    2. Stable
    3. Generating power
    4. Answers will vary

1																	2
H Hydrogen 1.008																	**He** Helium 4.003
3	4											5	6	7	8	9	10
Li Lithium 6.941	**Be** Beryllium 9.012											**B** Boron 10.81	**C** Carbon 12.01	**N** Nitrogen 14.01	**O** Oxygen 16.00	**F** Fluorine 19.00	**Ne** Neon 20.18
11	12											13	14	15	16	17	18
Na Sodium 22.99	**Mg** Magnesium 24.31											**Al** Aluminum 26.98	**Si** Silicon 28.09	**P** Phosphorus 30.97	**S** Sulfur 32.07	**Cl** Chlorine 35.45	**Ar** Argon 39.95
19	20	21	22	23	24	25	26	27	28	29	30	31	32	33	34	35	36
K Potassium 39.10	**Ca** Calcium 40.08	**Sc** Scandium 44.96	**Ti** Titanium 47.87	**V** Vanadium 50.94	**Cr** Chromium 52.00	**Mn** Manganese 54.94	**Fe** Iron 55.85	**Co** Cobalt 58.93	**Ni** Nickel 58.69	**Cu** Copper 63.55	**Zn** Zinc 65.39	**Ga** Gallium 69.72	**Ge** Germanium 72.61	**As** Arsenic 74.92	**Se** Selenium 78.96	**Br** Bromine 79.90	**Kr** Krypton 83.80
37	38	39	40	41	42	43	44	45	46	47	48	49	50	51	52	53	54
Rb Rubidium 85.47	**Sr** Strontium 87.62	**Y** Yttrium 88.91	**Zr** Zirconium 91.22	**Nb** Niobium 92.91	**Mo** Molybdenum 95.94	**Tc** Technetium 98.91	**Ru** Ruthenium 101.1	**Rh** Rhodium 102.9	**Pd** Palladium 106.4	**Ag** Silver 107.9	**Cd** Cadmium 112.4	**In** Indium 114.8	**Sn** Tin 118.7	**Sb** Antimony 121.8	**Te** Tellurium 127.6	**I** Iodine 126.9	**Xe** Xenon 131.3
55	56	* 71	72	73	74	75	76	77	78	79	80	81	82	83	84	85	86
Cs Cesium 132.9	**Ba** Barium 137.3	**Lu** Lutetium 175.0	**Hf** Hafnium 178.5	**Ta** Tantalum 181.0	**W** Tungsten 183.9	**Re** Rhenium 186.2	**Os** Osmium 190.2	**Ir** Iridium 192.2	**Pt** Platinum 195.1	**Au** Gold 197.0	**Hg** Mercury 200.6	**Tl** Thallium 204.4	**Pb** Lead 207.2	**Bi** Bismuth 209.0	**Po** Polonium [209]	**At** Astatine [210]	**Rn** Radon [222]
87	88	** 103	104	105	106	107	108	109	110	111	112	113	114	115	116	117	118
Fr Francium [223]	**Ra** Radium [226]	**Lr** Lawrencium [262]	**Rf** Rutherfordium [261]	**Db** Dubnium [262]	**Sg** Seaborgium [266]	**Bh** Bohrium [264]	**Hs** Hassium [269]	**Mt** Meitnerium [268]	**Ds** Darmstadtium [272]	**Rg** Roentgenium [272]	**Cn** Copernicium [285]	**Nh** Nihonium [286]	**Fl** Flerovium [289]	**Mc** Moscovium [289]	**Lv** Livermorium [293]	**Ts** Tennessine [294]	**Og** Oganesson [294]

*Lanthanides

57	58	59	60	61	62	63	64	65	66	67	68	69	70
La Lanthanum 138.9	**Ce** Cerium 140.1	**Pr** Praseodymium 140.9	**Nd** Neodymium 144.2	**Pm** Promethium [145]	**Sm** Samarium 150.4	**Eu** Europium 152.0	**Gd** Gadolinium 157.3	**Tb** Terbium 158.9	**Dy** Dysprosium 162.5	**Ho** Holmium 164.9	**Er** Erbium 167.3	**Tm** Thulium 168.9	**Yb** Ytterbium 173.0

**Actinides

89	90	91	92	93	94	95	96	97	98	99	100	101	102
Ac Actinium [227]	**Th** Thorium 232.0	**Pa** Protactinium 231.0	**U** Uranium 238.0	**Np** Neptunium [237]	**Pu** Plutonium [244]	**Am** Americium [243]	**Cm** Curium [247]	**Bk** Berkelium [247]	**Cf** Californium [251]	**Es** Einsteinium [252]	**Fm** Fermium [257]	**Md** Mendelevium [258]	**No** Nobelium [259]

Chemistry for the Grammar Stage

Physical Changes Unit

Physical Changes Unit Overview
(4 weeks)

Books Scheduled
📖 *Usborne Science Encyclopedia*

{Optional Encyclopedias}
📖 *Basher Science Chemistry*
📖 *Usborne Children's Encyclopedia*
📖 *DK Children's Encyclopedia*

Sequence for Study
➪ **Week 1:** States of Matter
➪ **Week 2:** Changes in State
➪ **Week 3:** Liquid Behavior
➪ **Week 4:** Gas Behavior

Physical Changes Poem to Memorize

<u>States of Matter</u>
Three states of matter
Solid, liquid, gas
Molecules scatter
As heat enters mass

A solid is firm
Atoms locked in tight
No room found to squirm
We can take a bite

Liquid moves freely
Atoms flow and gush
Filling easily
Even helps you flush

A gas has no shape
Moves without control
It tries to escape
Out every hole

Supplies Needed for the Unit

Week	Supplies needed
1	3 Balloons, Ice, Water
2	Orange juice, Cup
3	Pepper, Dish soap, Bowl, Water
4	Empty aluminum can, Bowl, Hot water, Ice, Tongs, Pan

Unit Vocabulary

1. **States of Matter** – The different forms in which a substance can exist: solid, liquid, and gas.
2. **Volume** – The space occupied by matter.
3. **Physical Change** – A change that occurs in which no new substances are made.
4. **Sublimation** – A change from solid to gas without going through liquid form.
5. **Surface Tension** – A force that pulls together molecules on the surface of a liquid.
6. **Evaporation** – The process by which the surface molecules of a liquid escape into a vapor.
7. **Diffusion** – The spreading out of a gas to fill the available space.

Week 1: States of Matter Lesson Plans

2-Days-a-week Schedule		
	Day 1	**Day 2**
Read	❏ Read "Solids, Liquids, and Gases, Part 1" ❏ {Choose one or more of the additional resources to read from this week}	❏ Read "Solids, Liquids, and Gases, Part 2" ❏ {Work on memorizing the "States of Matter" poem}
Do	❏ {Make a States of Matter Float or Work on the Physical Changes Poster}	❏ Do the Scientific Demonstration: Playing with Matter
Write	❏ Add information about states of matter to the students' notebook or lapbook ❏ Define states of matter and volume	❏ Add information about states of matter to the students' notebook or lapbook ❏ Complete the demonstration sheet ❏ {Work on the Physical Changes Weekly Review Sheet 1}

5-Days-a-week Schedule					
	Day 1	**Day 2**	**Day 3**	**Day 4**	**Day 5**
Read	❏ Read "Solids, Liquids, and Gases, Part 1"	❏ Read "Solids, Liquids, and Gases, Part 2"	❏ {Work on memorizing the "States of Matter" poem}	❏ {Choose one or more of the additional resources to read from this week}	❏ {Choose one or more of the additional resources to read from this week}
Do	❏ {Make a States of Matter Float}	❏ {Do some Liquid Observations}	❏ Do the Scientific Demonstration: Playing with Matter	❏ {Make a Gas Poster}	❏ {Work on the Physical Changes Poster}
Write	❏ Add information about states of matter to the students' notebook or lapbook	❏ Add information about states of matter to the students' notebook or lapbook	❏ Complete the demonstration sheet	❏ Define states of matter and volume	❏ {Work on the Physical Changes Weekly Review Sheet 1}

{These assignments are optional.}

Read – Information Gathering

Reading Assignments

❑ *Usborne Science Encyclopedia* p. 16 "Solids, Liquids, and Gases, Part 1"
   ? What are the three main forms that substances can be in?
   ? Do you remember what the kinetic theory is?

❑ *Usborne Science Encyclopedia* p. 17 "Solids, Liquids, and Gases, Part 2"
   ? What is volume?
   ? Can you tell me what density is?

Additional Explanantion: The Fourth State of Matter

There is also a fourth state of matter, plasma, which is a bit more abstract. It consists of atoms that have been split by high heat or electricity. Since it is difficult for students to be able to visualize plasma, we have left this information out for their first look at the different states of matter.

{Optional} Memory Work

 This week, begin memorizing the *States of Matter* poem. (SW p. 122)

{Optional} Additional Resources

Encyclopedias

 Basher Science Chemistry p. 8 "Solid"
 Usborne Children's Encyclopedia pp. 188-189 "Solids, liquids, and gases"
 DK Children's Encyclopedia p. 191 "Solid"

Library Books

 What Is the World Made Of? All About Solids, Liquids, and Gases (Let's-Read-and-Find... Science, Stage 2) by Kathleen Weidner Zoehfeld and Paul Meisel
 Solids, Liquids, And Gases (Rookie Read-About Science) by Ginger Garrett
 States of Matter: A Question and Answer Book by Fiona Bayrock and Anne McMullen

Do – Demonstration and Activities

Demonstration – Playing with Matter

You will need the following:
✓ 3 Balloons
✓ Water
✓ Ice

Demonstration Instructions

1. Read the following introduction to the students.

   In this unit, we are going to look at the physical changes that a substance can go through and how those substances tend to behave. Substances or matter can be found in three main forms, or states. Solids, liquids, and gases—we call these the three states of matter. In today's demonstration, we are going to look at water in these three states.

2. Fill one balloon with a solid (ice), one balloon with a liquid (water), and one with a gas (water vapor from your breath).
3. Let the students explore each of the balloons and observe the differences. As they make their observations, ask them questions such as:
   ? Which one floats the best?
   ? Which one is easiest to control?
   ? Which one has the most interesting shape?
4. Read the demonstration explanation to the students and have the students complete the demonstration sheet on SW p. 51.

Demonstration Explanation

The purpose of this demonstration was for the students to feel the differences between the three states of matter. When they are done, read the following to them:

> We saw that each balloon felt and behaved differently. Even though they were all filled with water, the water inside was in different states. The ice was the solid, the water was the liquid, and our breath acted as the water vapor. The three states of matter have very different physical properties and can behave differently, even when they are all composed of the same chemical substance.

{Optional} Unit Project

✄ **Physical Changes Poster** – During this unit, the students will create a poster depicting the physical changes that substances can go through. This week, have the students divide the poster into three sections. Place solids on the left, liquids in the center, and gases on the right. (**Note**–*This has been done for you in the SW on p. 48.*)

{Optional} Projects for This Week

✄ **States of Matter Float** – Make a States of Matter float with your students! You will need ice cream, root beer (or other type of soda), and a glass. Have the students add the solid (ice cream) first. Then, pour over the liquid (root beer) and watch the gas bubbles appear!

✄ **Liquid Observations** – Have the students observe liquids (a.k.a. water play). Provide a bucket and several different sizes of cups for the students to pour and fill. Then, let them loose!

✄ **Gas Poster** – Have the students make a poster depicting how the molecules behave in different states of matter. You will need a pencil, paint, and a sheet of paper. Divide a sheet into three parts and label the sections with solid, liquid, and gas. Then, draw a glass or beaker shape in each section. Have the students use the eraser end of the pencil to dip into the paint and then stamp molecules right next to each other in tightly-packed rows within the solid's beaker. Next, have the students stamp molecules slightly apart from each other within the liquid's beaker. Finally, have the students stamp molecules way apart from each other and even a few escaping from the gas's beaker.

Write - Notebooking

Writing Assignments
- **Student Workbook** – Have the students dictate, copy, or write two to four sentences on states of matter on SW p. 50.
- **{Optional} Lapbooking Templates** – Have the students begin the Physical and Chemical Changes lapbook by cutting out and coloring the cover on LT p. 34.
- **{Optional} Lapbooking Templates** – Have the students complete the States of Matter Cut-flap Book on LT p. 35. Have them cut out and fold the template. Have the students color the pictures on the cover. Then, have the students write the definition for solid, liquid, and gas on the inside. Finally, glue the flap-book into the lapbook.
- **{Optional} Coloring Pages** – Have the students color the following pages: Solids CP p. 26, Liquids CP p. 27, Gases CP p. 28.

Vocabulary
Have the students look up and copy the definitions for the following words:
- **States of Matter** – The different forms in which a substance can exist: solid, liquid, and gas. (SW p. 117)
- **Volume** – The space occupied by matter. (SW p. 118)

{Optional} Weekly Review Sheet
- "Physical Changes Weekly Review Sheet 1" on SW p. 151.
  Answers:
  1. B, C, A
  2. True
  3. False (*The molecules in a gas have more energy than the molecules in a solid.*)
  4. Answers will vary

Week 2: Changes in State Lesson Plans

2-Days-a-week Schedule		
	Day 1	**Day 2**
Read	❏ Read "Changes in Stage, Part 1" ❏ {Choose one or more of the additional resources to read from this week}	❏ Read "Changes in Stage, Part 2" ❏ {Work on memorizing the "States of Matter" poem}
Do	❏ {Do the Changes in State activity or Work on the Physical Changes Poster}	❏ Do the Scientific Demonstration: Freezy Meltdown
Write	❏ Add information about changes in state to the students' notebook or lapbook ❏ Define physical change and sublimation	❏ Add information about changes in state to the students' notebook or lapbook ❏ Complete the demonstration sheet ❏ {Work on the Physical Changes Weekly Review Sheet 2}

5-Days-a-week Schedule					
	Day 1	**Day 2**	**Day 3**	**Day 4**	**Day 5**
Read	❏ Read "Changes in Stage, Part 1"	❏ Read "Changes in Stage, Part 2"	❏ {Work on memorizing the "States of Matter" poem}	❏ {Choose one or more of the additional resources to read from this week}	❏ {Choose one or more of the additional resources to read from this week}
Do	❏ {Do the Changes in State activity}		❏ Do the Scientific Demonstration: Freezy Meltdown	❏ {Work on the Physical Changes Poster}	
Write	❏ Add information about changes in state to the students' notebook or lapbook	❏ Add information about changes in state to the students' notebook or lapbook	❏ Complete the demonstration sheet	❏ Define physical change and sublimation	❏ {Work on the Physical Changes Weekly Review Sheet 2}

Read – Information Gathering

Reading Assignments

- ❑ *Usborne Science Encyclopedia* p. 18 "Changes in State, Part 1"
    - **?** What happens when a solid melts (melting point)?
    - **?** What happens when a liquid boils (boiling point)?
- ❑ *Usborne Science Encyclopedia* p. 19 "Changes in State, Part 2"
    - **?** Do you remember what happens when a gas condenses?
    - **?** Do you remember what happens when a liquid freezes?

{Optional} Memory Work

- This week, begin memorizing the *States of Matter* poem. (SW p. 122)

{Optional} Additional Resources

Encyclopedias
- *Basher Science Chemistry* p. 14 "Melting Point," p. 15 "Boiling Point"
- *Usborne Children's Encyclopedia* p. 190 "How materials change, part 1"
- *DK Children's Encyclopedia* p. 194 "Changing States"

Library Books
- *How Water Changes (Weekly Reader: Science)* by Jim Mezzanotte
- *Solids (States of Matter)* by Jim Mezzanotte
- *Liquids (States of Matter)* by Jim Mezzanotte
- *Gases (States of Matter)* Jim Mezzanotte

Do – Demonstration and Activities

Demonstration – Freezy Meltdown

You will need the following:
- ✓ Orange juice (*Or other juice that your students like to drink.*)
- ✓ Cup

Demonstration Instructions

1. Read the following introduction to the students.

    Last week, we learned about the three states of matter–solids, liquids, and gases. A substance doesn't always stay in the same state. It can change states when it is heated or cooled. In today's demonstration, we are going to see these changes in state in action.

2. Pour a bit of juice in a cup for each of the students and have them take a sip of the juice.
3. Have the students place the remaining juice in the freezer.
4. After it has hardened (about an hour or two), take the cup out and have the students observe the changes that have occurred.

5. Let the cup sit on the counter in a place where it won't be disturbed.
6. After the juice has melted (about an hour or two), have the students take a sip of the juice to see if it tastes the same as it did during step 1.
7. Read the demonstration explanation to the students and have the students complete the demonstration sheet on SW p. 53.

Demonstration Explanation

The purpose of this demonstration was for the students see that freezing and melting are both physical changes. When they are done, read the following to them:

> We saw that the juice tastes the same at the beginning as it did at the end. We also saw that the juice became solid and did not pour after time in the freezer, and that it became a liquid again after it sat out on the counter. These changes were physical changes, which means that although the physical properties of the juice (liquid or solid) changed, the chemical make-up (the taste) did not. Changes in state, going from a liquid to a solid and vice versa, are known as physical changes.

{Optional} Take the Demonstration Further

Have the students repeat the process using different types of liquids to see if the results vary.

{Optional} Unit Project

✂ **Physical Changes Poster** – This week, have the students add the arrows for the physical changes they have learned about (melting, boiling, freezing, and condensing). Also, have them add pictures of solids or draw examples of solids under the "Solid" category.

{Optional} Projects for This Week

✂ **Changes in State** – Have the students set several ice cubes on a plate and set the plate out in the hot sun. Check the plate every five minutes to observe what happens. The students should see the solid water (ice) melt into liquid water, which then evaporates into a gas and disappears into the air.

Write – Notebooking

Writing Assignments

☐ **Student Workbook** – Have the students dictate, copy, or write two to four sentences on changes in state on SW p. 52.

☐ **{Optional} Lapbooking Templates** – Have the students complete the Changes in State Arrow-book on LT p. 36. Have the students cut out and fold the template. Have them color the picture on the cover. Then, have the students write several sentences about what they have learned. Finally, glue the flap-book into the lapbook.

☐ **{Optional} Coloring Pages** – Have the students color the following pages: Changes in Stage CP p. 29.

Vocabulary

Have the students look up and copy the definitions for the following words:
- **Physical Change** – A change that occurs in which no new substances are made. (SW p. 115)
- **Sublimation** – A change from solid to gas without going through liquid form. (SW p. 117)

{Optional} Weekly Review Sheet

- "Physical Changes Weekly Review Sheet 2" on SW p. 152.

    Answers:
    1. Melts, Boils
    2. Freezes, Condenses
    3. Answers will vary

Week 3: Liquid Behavior Lesson Plans

2-Days-a-week Schedule		
	Day 1	Day 2
Read	❑ Read "How Liquids Behave, Part 1" ❑ {Choose one or more of the additional resources to read from this week}	❑ Read "How Liquids Behave, Part 2" ❑ {Work on memorizing the "States of Matter" poem}
Do	❑ {Do the Water on a Penny activity or Work on the Physical Changes Poster}	❑ Do the Scientific Demonstration: Liquid Surface
Write	❑ Add information about how liquids behave to the students' notebook or lapbook ❑ Define evaporation and surface tension	❑ Add information about how liquids behave to the students' notebook or lapbook ❑ Complete the demonstration sheet ❑ {Work on the Physical Changes Weekly Review Sheet 3}

5-Days-a-week Schedule					
	Day 1	Day 2	Day 3	Day 4	Day 5
Read	❑ Read "How Liquids Behave, Part 1"	❑ Read "How Liquids Behave, Part 2"	❑ {Work on memorizing the "States of Matter" poem}	❑ {Choose one or more of the additional resources to read from this week}	❑ {Choose one or more of the additional resources to read from this week}
Do	❑ {Do the Liquid Behavior activity}	❑ {Watch Evaporation}	❑ Do the Scientific Demonstration: Liquid Surface	❑ {Do the Water on a Penny activity}	❑ {Work on the Physical Changes Poster}
Write	❑ Add information about how liquids behave to the students' notebook or lapbook	❑ Add information about how liquids behave to the students' notebook or lapbook	❑ Complete the demonstration sheet	❑ Define evaporation and surface tension	❑ {Work on the Physical Changes Weekly Review Sheet 3}

Read – Information Gathering

Reading Assignments

- ❑ *Usborne Science Encyclopedia* p. 20 "How Liquids Behave, Part 1"
    - ? Can a liquid change shape? Volume?
    - ? What happens as a liquid heats up?
    - ? What affects the rate of evaporation of a liquid?

- ❑ *Usborne Science Encyclopedia* p. 21 "How Liquids Behave, Part 2"
    - ? What is surface tension?
    - ? Do you remember what cohesion is?
    - ? Do you remember what adhesion is?

{Optional} Memory Work

- This week, begin memorizing the *States of Matter* poem. (SW p. 122)

{Optional} Additional Resources

Encyclopedias
- *Basher Science Chemistry* p. 10 "Liquid"
- *DK Children's Encyclopedia* p. 192 "Liquid"

Library Books
- *What Is a Liquid?* (First Step Nonfiction, States of Matter) by Jennifer Boothroyd
- *How Do You Measure Liquids?* (A+ Books: Measure It!) by Thomas K. Adamson
- *Saving Water: The Water Cycle* (Do It Yourself) by Buffy Silverman
- *Why Do Puddles Disappear?: Noticing Forms of Water* by Martha E. H. Rustad and Christine M. Schneider

Do – Demonstration and Activities

Demonstration – Liquid Surface

You will need the following:
- ✓ Ground Pepper
- ✓ Dish soap
- ✓ Bowl
- ✓ Water

Demonstration Instructions

1. Read the following introduction to the students.

    Last week, we learned about how a substance can change state from a solid to a liquid or from a liquid to a gas. This week, we are going to look closer at how liquids like to behave. One of the ways liquids act is to form a kind of stretchy skin on the surface of the liquid. In today's demonstration, we are going

to use pepper to see that stretchy skin and then do something to break it.
2. Fill the bowl about halfway with water and let it sit on a surface until the water stills.
3. Have the students gently sprinkle some pepper on the surface of the water and observe what the pepper does and add a picture or drawing to the demonstration sheet on SW p. 55.
4. Once the water stills, drop a drop of dish detergent into the water. Have the students observe what happens and add a picture or a drawing to the demonstration sheet before completing the sheet. As they draw, read the demonstration explanation to them.

Demonstration Explanation

The purpose of this demonstration was for the students to see what surface tension in water looks like. When they are done, read the following to them:

> We saw that at first the pepper floated on the surface of the water. It seemed like there was a stretchy skin that prevented it from falling to the bottom of the bowl. This stretchy skin is called surface tension. Surface tension is a force that pulls together the molecules found on the surface of a liquid, causing them to form a kind of skin. When the soap touches the water, it causes these connections to break. This allows the pepper to fall to the bottom of the bowl.

{Optional} Take the Demonstration Further

Have the students repeat the demonstration with a fresh bowl of water, only this time use a toothpick, pin, and/or a needle instead of the pepper.

{Optional} Unit Project

✕ **Physical Changes Poster** – This week, have the students add pictures of liquids or draw examples of liquids under the "Liquid" category.

{Optional} Projects for This Week

✕ **Liquid Behavior** – Complete the activity suggested on p. 21 of the *Usborne Science Encyclopedia*.

✕ **Evaporation** – Mix together a quarter cup of warm water and a tablespoon of salt. Pour the mixture into a shallow dish and set the dish out in a sunny place. Check the dish every hour or so to observe what happens.

✕ **Water on a Penny** – Have the students do the STEM challenge on surface tension using a penny, an eyedropper, and water. Lay the penny on a flat surface and fill the eyedropper with water. Have the students slowly add water to the top of the penny, one drop at a time. Thanks to surface tension, a bubble of water will form on the top of the penny. Have the students count how many drops it takes before the bubble breaks! (*The breakage will probably happen around 20 or so drops.*)

Write - Notebooking

Writing Assignments

- ☐ **Student Workbook** – Have the students dictate, copy, or write two to four sentences on how liquids behave on SW p. 54.
- ☐ **{Optional} Lapbooking Templates** – Have the students begin the How States Behave Tab-book on LT p. 37. Have them cut out the pages. Have the students color the pictures on the cover. This week, have them write their narration on the liquid tab. They can include information on how liquids behave, evaporation, and surface tension. Then, set the pages aside for next week.
- ☐ **{Optional} Coloring Pages** – Have the students color the following pages: Evaporation CP p. 30, Surface Tension CP p. 31.

Vocabulary

Have the students look up and copy the definitions for the following words:

- **Evaporation** – The process by which the surface molecules of a liquid escape into a vapor. (SW p. 110)
- **Surface Tension** – A force that pulls together molecules on the surface of a liquid. (SW p. 118)

{Optional} Weekly Review Sheet

- "Physical Changes Weekly Review Sheet 3" on SW p. 153.

    Answers:
    1. Shape, Volume
    2. False (*The hotter a liquid gets, the quicker it evaporates.*)
    3. True
    4. Answers will vary

Week 4: Gas Behavior Lesson Plans

2-Days-a-week Schedule		
	Day 1	Day 2
Read	❑ Read "How Gases Behave, Part 1" and the "Section on Brownian Motion" ❑ {Choose one or more of the additional resources to read from this week}	❑ Read "How Gases Behave, Part 2" ❑ {Work on memorizing the "States of Matter" poem}
Do	❑ {Do the Gas Diffusion activity or Work on the Physical Changes Poster}	❑ Do the Scientific Demonstration: Can Crusher
Write	❑ Add information about how gases behave to the students' notebook or lapbook ❑ Define diffusion	❑ Add information about how gases behave to the students' notebook or lapbook ❑ Complete the demonstration sheet ❑ {Work on the Physical Changes Weekly Review Sheet 4}

5-Days-a-week Schedule					
	Day 1	Day 2	Day 3	Day 4	Day 5
Read	❑ Read "How Gases Behave, Part 1"	❑ Read "How Gases Behave, Part 2"	❑ {Work on memorizing the "States of Matter" poem}	❑ Read "Section on Brownian Motion"	❑ {Choose one or more of the additional resources to read from this week}
Do	❑ {Do the Gas Diffusion activity}	❑ {Work on the Physical Changes Poster}	❑ Do the Scientific Demonstration: Can Crusher	❑ {Create a Brownian Painting}	❑ {Work on the Physical Changes Poster}
Write	❑ Add information about how gases behave to the students' notebook or lapbook	❑ Add information about how gases behave to the students' notebook or lapbook	❑ Complete the demonstration sheet	❑ Define diffusion	❑ {Work on the Physical Changes Weekly Review Sheet 4}

Read – Information Gathering

Reading Assignments

- ❑ *Usborne Science Encyclopedia* p. 22 "How Gases Behave, Part 1"
  - ? What happens in diffusion?
  - ? Do you remember where molecules want to move?
- ❑ *Usborne Science Encyclopedia* p. 23 "How Gases Behave, Part 2"
  - ? What is pressure?
  - ? Can you tell me what happens when you heat a substance up?
- ❑ *Usborne Science Encyclopedia* p. 16 "Section on Brownian Motion"
  - ? What is Brownian motion?

{Optional} Memory Work

- This week, begin memorizing the *States of Matter* poem. (SW p. 122)

{Optional} Additional Resources

Encyclopedias
- *Basher Science Chemistry* p. 12 "Gas," p. 14 "Brownian Motion"
- *DK Children's Encyclopedia* p. 193 "Gases"

Library Books
- *What Is a Gas? (First Step Nonfiction)* by Jennifer Boothroyd
- *It's a Gas!* by Ruth Griffin, Margaret Griffin and Pat Cupples

Do – Demonstration and Activities

Demonstration – Can Crusher

You will need the following:
- ✓ Empty aluminum can
- ✓ Bowl
- ✓ Hot water
- ✓ Ice
- ✓ Tongs

Demonstration Instructions

1. Read the following introduction to the students.

    Last week, we learned how liquid behave and what surface tension is. This week, we are going to look at how gases behave. Gases have no definite shape or volume. They like to fill up the all of the space of the container they are in. Gases push against the edges of the container they are in all the time. We call this exerting pressure. In today's demonstration, we going to see what happens when the pressure inside a can changes.

2. Have the students fill a bowl halfway with ice water.
3. **(Adults Only)** Then, add about a third of a cup of very hot water to the cans. (*There should be steam coming out of the top of the can.*)
4. Have the students briefly observe what happens to the shape of the can after adding the hot water.
5. **(Adults Only)** While the can is still steaming, use the tongs to pick up the can and place it upside down into the other bowl of ice. (*The opening of the can should be submerged.*)
6. Have the students observe what happens to the can. When they are done, read the demonstration explanation to them and have them complete the demonstration sheet on SW p. 57.

Demonstration Explanation

The purpose of this demonstration was for the students to see the effects of the pressure a gas exerts. When they are done, read the following to them:

> We saw that when I added the hot water to the can, the shape stayed the same. There was a bit of gas, or steam that escaped from the opening, but the can didn't change. When I flipped the can over and placed it into the ice water, something did happen! The can shrank in on itself. This is because as the gas cools, part of it condenses and the remaining gas takes up less space. Because no more air can come into the can, the pressure the remaining gas pushes with is less and the can shrinks!

{Optional} Take the Demonstration Further

Blow up a balloon and have the students measure the diameter. Then, place the balloon in the freezer for thirty minutes. Take the balloon out and have the students measure the diameter once more. Did it change? (*The students should see that the diameter of the balloon shrank, as the pressure the gas exerts on the ballon decreases as it cools, just like in the demonstration.*)

{Optional} Unit Project

✂ **Physical Changes Poster** – This week, have the students add pictures of gases or draw examples of gases under the "Gas" category.

{Optional} Projects for This Week

✂ **Gas Diffusion** – Have the students use their noses to detect the diffusion of gases. You will need vanilla extract, an eyedropper, and a cotton ball. Place a few drops of vanilla extract on the cotton ball and then wait for a few minutes. Have the students raise their hands as soon as they can smell the vanilla. (*The students are able to smell the vanilla as the molecules of vanilla gas move, or diffuse, through the air to reach their noses.*)

✂ **Brownian Painting** – Have the students create a Brownian motion painting. You will need a small ball (marble or rubber bouncy ball), paint, paper, and a tray. Place the paper in the tray. Then, have the students dip the ball into the paint and place it in the tray. Have them pick up the tray and shake it gently with random motions. The ball will move around and create random paths similar to the Brownian motion of a molecule in a liquid or gas.

Write – Notebooking

Writing Assignments
- ☐ **Student Workbook –** Have the students dictate, copy, or write two to four sentences on how gases behave on SW p. 56.
- ☐ **{Optional} Lapbooking Templates –** Have the students begin the How States Behave Tab-book on LT p. 37. Have them cut out the pages. Have the students color the pictures on the cover. This week, have them write their narration on the liquid tab. They can include information on how gases behave, diffusion, and pressure/temperature. Then, set the pages aside for next week.
- ☐ **{Optional} Coloring Pages –** Have the students color the following pages: Diffusion CP p. 32.

Vocabulary
Have the students look up and copy the definition for the following word:
- **Diffusion –** The spreading out of a gas to fill the available space. (SW p. 109)

{Optional} Weekly Review Sheet
- "Physical Changes Weekly Review Sheet 4" on SW p. 154.
    Answers:
    1. True
    2. High, Low
    3. Pressure
    4. Answers will vary

Chemistry for the Grammar Stage

Chemical Changes Unit

Chemical Changes Unit Overview
(4 weeks)

Books Scheduled
📖 *Usborne Science Encyclopedia*

{Optional Encyclopedias}
📖 *Basher Science Chemistry*
📖 *Usborne Children's Encyclopedia*

Sequence for Study
↪ **Week 1:** Bonding
↪ **Week 2:** Chemical Reactions
↪ **Week 3:** Types of Reactions
↪ **Week 4:** Oxidation and Reduction

Chemical Changes Poem to Memorize

Reactions
Atoms bump into each other in space
Bonding—connecting at a rapid pace
These compounds form in three main types of bonds
Different ways electrons correspond
In an ionic bond, one atom asks
The other gives electrons to the task
In a covalent bond the atoms share
Electrons joined in a happy pair
The metallic bond is a little strange
Electrons swirl in a constant exchange
This bonding happens in a reaction
Reactants to products—one cool action
As this tidy chemical change occurs
The mass stays the same, it only transfers
Exothermic reactions give off heat
Endothermic ones cool as atoms meet
Catalysts help by speeding up the pace
Redox is when electrons swap their place

Supplies Needed for the Unit

Week	Supplies needed
1	Salt, Magnifying glass, Warm water, Cup, Spoon
2	Shallow dish, Paper towel, Bowl, Vinegar, Pennies
3	Baking soda, Vinegar, Water, Epsom salts, 2 Cups
4	Apple, Cotton ball, Lemon juice

Unit Vocabulary

1. **Chemical Bond** – A force that holds together two or more atoms.
2. **Chemical Reaction** – An occurrence where the atoms in substances are rearranged to form new substances.
3. **Catalyst** – A substance that speeds up a chemical reaction.
4. **Enzyme** – A catalyst that speeds up a chemical reaction in living things.
5. **Redox Reaction** – A chemical reaction that involves the transfer of electrons.

Week 1: Bonding Lesson Plans

2-Days-a-week Schedule		
	Day 1	**Day 2**
Read	❏ Read "Bonding, Part 1 and Part 2" ❏ {Choose one or more of the additional resources to read from this week}	❏ Read "Bonding, Part 3" ❏ {Work on memorizing the "Reactions" poem}
Do	❏ {Create an artisitc version of one of the types of bonds or Work on the Chemical Changes Poster}	❏ Do the Scientific Demonstration: Bond Breaking
Write	❏ Add information about bonding to the students' notebook or lapbook ❏ Define chemical bond	❏ Add information about bonding to the students' notebook or lapbook ❏ Complete the demonstration sheet ❏ {Work on the Chemical Changes Weekly Review Sheet 1}

5-Days-a-week Schedule					
	Day 1	**Day 2**	**Day 3**	**Day 4**	**Day 5**
Read	❏ Read "Bonding, Part 1"	❏ Read "Bonding, Part 2"	❏ {Work on memorizing the "Reactions" poem}	❏ Read "Bonding, Part 3"	❏ {Choose one or more of the additional resources to read from this week}
Do	❏ {Create an artistic version of ionic bonds}	❏ {Create an artistic version of convalent bonds}	❏ Do the Scientific Demonstration: Bond Breaking	❏ {Create an artistic version of metallic bonds}	❏ {Work on the Chemical Changes Poster}
Write	❏ Add information about bonding to the students' notebook or lapbook	❏ Add information about bonding to the students' notebook or lapbook	❏ Complete the demonstration sheet ❏ Define chemical bond	❏ Add information about bonding to the students' notebook or lapbook	❏ {Work on the Chemical Changes Weekly Review Sheet 1}

{These assignments are optional.}

Read – Information Gathering

Reading Assignments

- ❏ *Usborne Science Encyclopedia* p. 68 "Bonding, Part 1"
    - ? What is bonding in chemistry?
    - ? Do you remember how electron shells are involved in bonding?
- ❏ *Usborne Science Encyclopedia* p. 69 "Bonding, Part 2"
    - ? Can you tell me how a covalent bond forms?
    - ? What types of elements form a covalent bond?
    - ? What is a giant molecule?
- ❏ *Usborne Science Encyclopedia* p. 70 "Bonding, Part 3"
    - ? Can you tell me how an ionic bond forms?
    - ? What types of elements form an ionic bond?
    - ? Can you tell me how a metallic bond forms?
    - ? What types of elements form a metallic bond?

{Optional} Memory Work

- This week, begin memorizing the *Reactions* poem. (SW p. 123)

{Optional} Additional Resources

Encyclopedias

- *Basher Science Chemistry* p. 30 "Ions," p. 34 "Giant molecules," p. 36 "Metallic bonding"
- *Usborne Science Encyclopedia* p. 71 "Valency and Allotropes"

Library Books

There are no additional books on the market for these topics. Instead, you can watch the following videos on bonding:
- Covalent bonding - https://www.youtube.com/watch?v=LkAykOv1foc
- Ionic bonding - https://www.youtube.com/watch?v=DEdRcfyYnSQ
- Chemical bonding - https://www.youtube.com/watch?v=_M9khs87xQ8

Do – Demonstration and Activities

Demonstration – Bond Breaking

You will need the following:
- ✓ Salt
- ✓ Magnifying glass
- ✓ Warm water
- ✓ Cup
- ✓ Spoon

Demonstration Instructions

1. Read the following introduction to the students.

    In this unit, we are going to look at the chemical changes that atoms can go through. When atoms of an element meet an atom of another element, they can bond or join together. This week, we are going to look at the three major types of bonding: covalent, ionic, and metallic. In this demonstration, we are going to see what happens when the ionic bond between the sodium and the chlorine in salt is broken.

2. Pour out a small pile of salt (about half a teaspoon) onto the spoon. Have the students observe the crystals with the magnifying glass and draw what they see on the demonstration sheet on SW p. 63.
3. Meanwhile, fill the cup of water halfway with warm water. When the students are done with their observations, have them add the salt to the warm water and stir. Have them observe what happens and draw what they see on the demonstration sheet once the water settles.
4. Read the demonstration explanation to the students and have them complete the demonstration sheet.

Demonstration Explanation

The purpose of this demonstration was for the students to get a simplistic view of the change in a substance when the bonds are broken. When they are done, read the following to them:

   When we observed the salt all by itself, we saw which crystal cubes. These granuales are the result of the lattice structure that sodium and chlorine form when they bond together ionically. When we placed those crystals in the warm water, they disappeared. This is because there was enough energy and attraction from the water molecules to pull those ionic bonds apart.

{Optional} Take the Demonstration Further

Repeat the demonstration with other crystals in your kitchen, such as sugar, to see if the results are the same.

{Optional} Unit Project

✂ **Chemical Changes Poster** – Over the course of this unit, the students will create a poster about depicting the three types of bonding and the different chemical reactions. This week, have them divide the top half of their posters into three sections labeled—covalent, ionic, and metallic. Under each section the students can include how the type of bond is formed, what types of elements form that particular bond, and examples of substances that have that type of bonding. (**Note** – *This has been done for you in the SW on p. 60.*)

{Optional} Projects for This Week

✂ **Bonding Art** – Have the students learn about bonding by creating an artistic representation of the different types of bonds. You will need two colors of paint, paper, a few pompom balls,

and a pencil eraser. Here are the directions:
- **Ionic bonding** – Have the students dip a pompom in one color of paint and use it to make nine dots in two circles, two in a center circle and seven in a surrounding circle, leaving space for one more in the outer circle. Now take another pompom and dip in the other color of paint to make a dot in the space left in the outer circle you previously made, creating an artistic ionic bond.
- **Covalent bonding** – Have the students dip a pompom into one of the colors of paint and use it to make ten dots in two circles, two in a center circle, and eight in a surrounding circle. Then, have them cut a pompom in half and dip it into the other color of paint. Use the half pompom to paint over half of the two of the dots in the outer circle they made previously, creating an artistic covalent bond.
- **Metallic bonding** – Have the students dip a pompom into one of the colors of paint and then make a 4 by 3 grid on the paper. (*Be sure to leave space in the grid for the mini-dots.*) Then, have them dip the end of the pencil eraser into the other color of paint and use it to randomly scatter the mini-dots in between grid they made previously, creating an artistic metallic bond.

Write – Notebooking

Writing Assignments
- ☐ **Student Workbook** – Have the students dictate, copy, or write two to four sentences on bonding on SW p. 62.
- ☐ **{Optional} Lapbooking Templates** – Have the students complete the Bonding Triangle-book on LT p. 38. Have them cut out and fold the templates. Have the students color the cover and glue it on the outside. Then, have the students write the definitions for covalent, ionic, and metallic bonding on the inside. Finally, glue the triangle-book into the lapbook.
- ☐ **{Optional} Coloring Pages** – Have the students color the following pages: Bonding CP p. 33.

Vocabulary
Have the students look up and copy the definition for the following word:
- ✎ **Chemical Bond** – A force that holds together two or more atoms. (SW p. 107)

{Optional} Weekly Review Sheet
- ♩ "Chemical Changes Weekly Review Sheet 1" on SW p. 155.
    Answers:
    1. Ionic
    2. Metallic
    3. Covalent
    4. Answers will vary

Week 2: Chemical Reactions Lesson Plans

2-Days-a-week Schedule		
	Day 1	**Day 2**
Read	❑ Read "Chemical Reactions, Part 1" ❑ *{Choose one or more of the additional resources to read from this week}*	❑ Read "Chemical Reactions, Part 2" ❑ *{Work on memorizing the "Reactions" poem}*
Do	❑ *{Do the Chemical Reactions activity or Work on the Chemical Changes Poster}*	❑ Do the Scientific Demonstration: Penny Change
Write	❑ Add information about chemical reactions to the students' notebook or lapbook ❑ Define chemical reaction	❑ Add information about chemical reactions to the students' notebook or lapbook ❑ Complete the demonstration sheet ❑ *{Work on the Chemical Changes Weekly Review Sheet 2}*

5-Days-a-week Schedule					
	Day 1	**Day 2**	**Day 3**	**Day 4**	**Day 5**
Read	❑ Read "Chemical Reactions, Part 1"	❑ Read "Chemical Reactions, Part 2"	❑ *{Work on memorizing the "Reactions" poem}*	❑ *{Choose one or more of the additional resources to read from this week}*	❑ *{Choose one or more of the additional resources to read from this week}*
Do	❑ *{Do the Chemical Reactions activity}*	❑ *{Test the Conservation of Mass}*	❑ Do the Scientific Demonstration: Penny Change	❑ *{Have a Mole Day Celebration}*	❑ *{Work on the Chemical Changes Poster}*
Write	❑ Add information about chemical reactions to the students' notebook or lapbook	❑ Add information about chemical reactions to the students' notebook or lapbook	❑ Complete the demonstration sheet	❑ Define chemical reaction	❑ *{Work on the Chemical Changes Weekly Review Sheet 2}*

Read – Information Gathering

Reading Assignments

- ❑ *Usborne Science Encyclopedia* p. 76 "Chemical Reactions, Part 1"
    - ? What happens in a chemical reaction?
    - ? What are the reactants? What are the products?
- ❑ *Usborne Science Encyclopedia* p. 77 "Chemical Reactions, Part 2"
    - ? What is the law of conservation of mass?
    - ? Do you remember what a mole is and how chemists use it?

{Optional} Memory Work

- This week, begin memorizing the *Reactions* poem. (SW p. 123)

{Optional} Additional Resources

Encyclopedias

- *Basher Science Chemistry* p. 40 "Avogadro's number," p. 41 "Mole," p. 82 "Chemical Reaction"
- *Usborne Children's Encyclopedia* p. 191 "How materials change, part 2"

Library Books

There are no additional books on the market for these topics. Instead, you can watch the following video on chemical and physical changes:
- https://www.youtube.com/watch?v=BgM3e8YZxuc

Do – Demonstration and Activities

Demonstration – Penny Change

You will need the following:
- ✓ Shallow dish
- ✓ Paper towel
- ✓ Bowl
- ✓ Vinegar
- ✓ Pennies

Demonstration Instructions

1. Read the following introduction to the students.

    Last week, we talked about the different types of bonding. This week, we are going to learn about chemical reactions. In these reactions, bonds between atoms in a molecule are broken. Then, new bonds are formed with different atoms, creating one or more new molecules. In this demonstration, we are going to see this new molecule appear with a color change!

2. Fold the paper towel in half, set it on the dish, and pour enough vinegar on it to soak it.

3. Have the students set the pennies on the paper towel and then cover the paper towel with an overturned bowl. Set the plate in a place where it won't be disturbed and let it sit for at least 4 hours or up to 24 hours.
4. After the time has passed, have the students check the pennies and observe if there are any changes.
5. Read the demonstration explanation to the students and have the students complete the demonstration sheet on SW p. 65.

Demonstration Explanation

The purpose of this demonstration was for the students see a chemical change take place. When they are done, read the following to them:

> We saw the pennies change color. They went from copper color to green. It's not because of magic—it's science! It happens because of a chemical reaction between the copper coating and the vinegar. Vinegar is a chemical knowns as acetic acid. It reacts with the copper in the coating of the pennies and changes that coating. The reaction creates a new chemical that is green in color—copper acetate.

{Optional} Take the Demonstration Further

Have the students observe a chemical reaction with cleaning power. You will need several dull, dirty pennies, a cup, and a can of dark cola soda. Place the pennies in the cup and pour the soda over them. Let the cup sit overnight. The next morning pour out the soda and observe the changes. (*The pennies should come out bright and shiny. This is because the phosphoric acid in dark cola reacts with the dirty, oxidized dull, top layer on the penny and returns it to bright and shiny!*)

{Optional} Unit Project

✂ **Chemical Changes Poster** – This week, have the students add a chemical reaction to the middle of their poster. Have them label the reactants side and the products side above the equation. Under the equation, have the students write the definition of a chemical reaction.

{Optional} Projects for This Week

✂ **Chemical Reactions** – Have the students observe another chemical change by curdling milk. Add ¼ cup of vinegar to a clear glass or bowl. Then, add ¾ cup of milk and stir gently to mix. Wait fifteen minutes and observe the changes that have occurred. (*The acid in the vinegar causes the proteins to in the milk to bind up together, producing a chemical change that cannot be reversed.*)

✂ **Conservation of Mass** – Place a few ice cubes in a plastic cup and fill the cup ¾ of the way up with water. Use a maker to mark the water level and set the cup to the side. Keep checking the cup every hour until the ice completely melts to see how the water level changes. (*The students should see that the water level line doesn't change. This is due to the law of conservation of mass.*)

✂ **Mole Day** – Have a mole day celebration with you students. Traditionally, this would be done on June 23 or October 23, but you can celebrate Avogadro's number any day! Here are a few ideas you can use for your mole day celebration:
🖱 http://www.moleday.org/

Write – Notebooking

Writing Assignments
- ☐ **Student Workbook** – Have the students dictate, copy, or write two to four sentences on chemical reactions on SW p. 64.
- ☐ **{Optional} Lapbooking Templates** – Have the students complete the Reactions Mini-book on LT p. 39. Have the students cut out and fold the template. Have them color the picture on the cover. Then, have the students several sentences about what they have learned. Finally, glue the mini-book into the lapbook.
- ☐ **{Optional} Coloring Pages** – Have the students color the following pages: Chemical Reactions CP p. 34.

Vocabulary
Have the students look up and copy the definition for the following word:
- ✏ **Chemical Reaction** – An occurrence where the atoms in substances are rearranged to form new substances. (SW p. 108)

{Optional} Weekly Review Sheet
- 🖊 "Chemical Changes Weekly Review Sheet 2" on SW p. 156.
   Answers:
   1. Reactants, Products
   2. Stays the same
   3. True
   4. Answers will vary

Week 3: Types of Reactions Lesson Plans

2-Days-a-week Schedule		
	Day 1	**Day 2**
Read	❏ Read "Chemical Reactions, Part 3" ❏ {Choose one or more of the additional resources to read from this week}	❏ Read "Chemical Reactions, Part 4" ❏ {Work on memorizing the "Reactions" poem}
Do	❏ {Do the Catalyst Reaction or Work on the Chemical Changes Poster}	❏ Do the Scientific Demonstration: Types of Reactions
Write	❏ Add information about types of reaction to the students' notebook or lapbook ❏ Define catalyst and enzyme	❏ Add information about types of reaction to the students' notebook or lapbook ❏ Complete the demonstration sheet ❏ {Work on the Chemical Changes Weekly Review Sheet 3}

5-Days-a-week Schedule					
	Day 1	**Day 2**	**Day 3**	**Day 4**	**Day 5**
Read	❏ Read "Chemical Reactions, Part 3"	❏ Read "Chemical Reactions, Part 4"	❏ {Work on memorizing the "Reactions" poem}	❏ {Choose one or more of the additional resources to read from this week}	❏ {Choose one or more of the additional resources to read from this week}
Do	❏ {Have some Exothermic Fun}	❏ {Do the Catalyst Reaction}	❏ Do the Scientific Demonstration: Types of Reactions	❏ {Work on the Chemical Changes Poster}	
Write	❏ Add information about types of reaction to the students' notebook or lapbook	❏ Add information about types of reaction to the students' notebook or lapbook	❏ Complete the demonstration sheet	❏ Define catalyst and enzyme	❏ {Work on the Chemical Changes Weekly Review Sheet 3}

Read – Information Gathering

Reading Assignments

❑ *Usborne Science Encyclopedia* p. 78 "Chemical Reactions, Part 3"
   ? What is an endothermic reaction?
   ? What is an exothermic reaction?
   ? What is another type of reaction?

❑ *Usborne Science Encyclopedia* p. 79 "Chemical Reactions, Part 4"
   ? What is a catalyst?
   ? What is an enzyme?

{Optional} Memory Work
This week, begin memorizing the *Reactions* poem. (SW p. 123)

{Optional} Additional Resources
Encyclopedias
Basher Science Chemistry p. 88 "Activation Energy," p. 90 "Catalyst," p. 91 "Enzyme"

Library Books
There are no additional books on the market for these topics. Instead, you can watch the following video on catalysts:
https://www.youtube.com/watch?v=OttRV5ykP7A

Do – Demonstration and Activities

Demonstration – Types of Reactions
You will need the following:
- ✓ Baking soda
- ✓ Vinegar
- ✓ Water
- ✓ Epsom salts
- ✓ 2 Cups

Demonstration Instructions

1. Read the following introduction to the students.

   Last week we learned about chemical reactions. This week, we are learning about the different types of chemical reactions. These reactions can release heat or absorb heat. We have special names for this process. A reaction that releases heat is called exothermic. A reaction that absorbs heat is called endothermic. In today's demonstration, we are going to do two different reactions—can you guess which one is exothermic and which one is endothermic?

2. Pour a few tablespoons of vinegar in one of the cups and add a teaspoon of baking soda.

3. Have the students touch the outside of the cup and feel what happens to the temperature. Have them record their observations on the demonstration sheet on SW p. 67.
4. In the second cup, add several tablespoons of water and add a teaspoon of Epsom salts.
5. Have the students touch the outside of the cup and feel what happens to the temperature. Have them record their observations on the demonstration sheet.
6. Read the demonstration explanation to the students and have the students complete the demonstration sheet.

Demonstration Explanation

The purpose of this demonstration was for the students to feel two types of reactions—endothermic and exothermic. When they are done, read the following to them:

> In the first cup, we felt the cup get warmer when we mixed the baking soda and vinegar. This is because the reaction is exothermic, meaning that as baking soda and vinegar react heat is released. In the second cup, we felt the cup get cooler when we mixed the Epsom salts and water. This is because the reaction is endothermic, meaning that as Epsom salts and water react heat is absorbed.

{Optional} Take the Demonstration Further

Have the students repeat the demonstration with other materials. You can have them choose the materials or you can use Plaster of Paris and water, which is an exothermic reaction.

{Optional} Unit Project

- **Chemical Changes Poster** – This week, under the equation, have the students write the definition of a endothermic and exothermic reactions.

{Optional} Projects for This Week

- **Exothermic Fun** – Have the students do the "See for Yourself" activity on p. 79 of the *Usborne Science Encyclopedia*.
- **Catalyst Reaction** – Have the students watch a catalyst in action through the elephant toothpaste reaction! You will need a plastic bottle, small bowl, warm water, yeast, hydrogen peroxide, and dish soap for this demonstration. In a small bowl, mix ¼ cup of warm water with about a tablespoon of yeast and set aside. Pour about ½ a cup of hydrogen peroxide into the plastic bottle and add several drops of liquid dish soap. Next, quickly add the yeast mixture and step back to watch the toothpaste form!

Write – Notebooking

Writing Assignments

- ☐ **Student Workbook** – Have the students dictate, copy, or write two to four sentences on types of reactions on SW p. 66.
- ☐ **{Optional} Lapbooking Templates** – Have the students complete the Types of Reactions Sheet on LT p. 40. Have the students cut out the template. Have the students write several

sentences about what they have learned about endothermic and exothermic reactions. Then, have them glue the sheet into the lapbook.

- ☐ **{Optional} Coloring Pages** – Have the students color the following pages: Types of Reactions CP p. 35.

Vocabulary

Have the students look up and copy the definitions for the following words:
- **Catalyst** – A substance that speeds up a chemical reaction. (SW p. 107)
- **Enzyme** – A catalyst that speeds up a chemical reaction in living things. (SW p. 107)

{Optional} Weekly Review Sheet

- "Chemical Changes Weekly Review Sheet 3" on SW p. 157.

    Answers:
    1. Exothermic, Endothermic
    2. False (*A catalyst can speed up or slow down a reaction.*)
    3. Enzyme
    4. Answers will vary

Week 4: Oxidation and Reduction Lesson Plans

2-Days-a-week Schedule		
	Day 1	Day 2
Read	☐ Read "Oxidation and Reduction, Part 1" ☐ {Choose one or more of the additional resources to read from this week}	☐ Read "Oxidation and Reduction, Part 2" ☐ {Work on memorizing the "Reactions" poem}
Do	☐ {Learn about fireworks or Work on the Chemical Changes Poster}	☐ Do the Scientific Demonstration: Browning
Write	☐ Add information about oxidation and reduction to the students' notebook or lapbook ☐ Define redox reaction	☐ Add information about oxidation and reduction to the students' notebook or lapbook ☐ Complete the demonstration sheet ☐ {Work on the Chemical Changes Weekly Review Sheet 4}

5-Days-a-week Schedule					
	Day 1	Day 2	Day 3	Day 4	Day 5
Read	☐ Read "Oxidation and Reduction, Part 1"	☐ Read "Oxidation and Reduction, Part 2"	☐ {Work on memorizing the "Reactions" poem}	☐ {Choose one or more of the additional resources to read from this week}	☐ {Choose one or more of the additional resources to read from this week}
Do	☐ {Learn about fireworks}	☐ {Practice some Reduction Cleaning}	☐ Do the Scientific Demonstration: Browning	☐ {Work on the Chemical Changes Poster}	☐ {Review the work from the unit}
Write	☐ Add information about oxidation and reduction to the students' notebook or lapbook	☐ Add information about oxidation and reduction to the students' notebook or lapbook	☐ Complete the demonstration sheet	☐ Define redox reaction	☐ {Work on the Chemical Changes Weekly Review Sheet 4}

Read – Information Gathering

Reading Assignments

- ❑ *Usborne Science Encyclopedia* p. 80 "Oxidation and Reduction, Part 1"
    - **?** What is oxidation?
    - **?** Do you remember what happens during combustion?
- ❑ *Usborne Science Encyclopedia* p. 81 "Oxidation and Reduction, Part 2"
    - **?** What is reduction?
    - **?** Do you remember what happens during photosynthesis?

{Optional} Memory Work

- This week, begin memorizing the *Reactions* poem. (SW p. 123)

{Optional} Additional Resources

Encyclopedias

- *Basher Science Chemistry* p. 86 "Combustion," p. 89 "Fireworks"

Library Books

There are no additional books on the market for these topics. Instead, you can watch the following video on oxidation and reduction:

- https://www.youtube.com/watch?v=dF5lB7gRtcA

Do – Demonstration and Activities

Demonstration – Browning

You will need the following:
- ✓ Apple
- ✓ Cotton ball
- ✓ Lemon juice

Demonstration Instructions

1. Read the following introduction to the students.

    Last week we learned different types of reactions. This week, we are going to look at a specific type of reaction called a oxidation-reduction reaction, or redox for short. In this demonstration, we will see the oxidation happening before our very eyes!

2. **(Adults Only)** Cut the apple in half.
3. Have the students dip the cotton ball in lemon juice and rub the juice all over one half of the apple.
4. Set the apple halves aside in a place where they won't be disturbed.
5. Have the students check the apple halves every hour over the next four hours and have them make observations about the changes.

6. Have the students observe what happens. When they are done, read the demonstration explanation to the students and have them complete the demonstration sheet on SW p. 69.

Demonstration Explanation

The purpose of this demonstration was for the students to see an oxidation-reduction reaction in action. When they are done, read the following to them:

> We saw that the apple half with the lemon juice remains the same color, while the plain apple half begins to turn brown. This browning is due to a special type of a reaction called an oxidation-reduction reaction. In this chemical reaction the oxygen in the air begins to break down the cells in the apple, causing it to turn brown. The lemon juice on the half of the apple stopped this reaction from occuring.

{Optional} Take the Demonstration Further

Have the students look at another oxidation-reduction reaction: rusting. You can get the directions for this at the following website:

https://teachbesideme.com/oxidation-rust-experiment/

{Optional} Unit Project

- **Chemical Changes Poster** – This week, under the equation, have the students write the definition of oxidation and reduction reactions.

{Optional} Projects for This Week

- **Fireworks Oxidation** – Have the students learn about the chemistry of fireworks by watching the following video:

  https://www.youtube.com/watch?v=nPHegSulI_M

  Then, afterwards, you can make fireworks in a jar, which is not exactly an example of an oxidation reaction, but it is much safer to do in your kitchen! You will need food coloring, oil, a fork, a shallow bowl, warm water, and a glass jar. Pour a bit of oil in a bowl and add a few drops of food coloring. Break the drops into tiny droplets with a fork. Slowly add the oil mixture in a jar filled partway with water. Wait a moment and observe the fireworks!

- **Reduction Cleaning** – Have the students use a reduction reaction to clean a tarnished (oxidized) piece of silver. You will need a tarnished silver item (jewelry or silverware), tongs, a bowl, aluminum foil, baking soda, and hot water. Cover the bottom of the bowl with aluminum foil and then sprinkle 1 tablespoon of baking soda over it. Add a cup of hot water and mix until the baking soda is dissolved. Now, use the tongs to place the tarnished silver item into the solution. Wait a minute or two. (*You will see bubbles form and you might smell a rotten egg scent.*) Then, use the tongs to take the item out and observe the changes. (*The students should see that the item is much cleaner. This is because a redox reaction occurs between the aluminum, baking soda, and the tarnish, which is caused by a sulfur compound. This reaction removes the tarnish from the silver. Once the silver is exposed to the air again, sulfur in the air will cause another redox reaction, which produces the tarnish we see.*)

Write – Notebooking

Writing Assignments
- ☐ **Student Workbook** – Have the students dictate, copy, or write two to four sentences on oxidation and reduction on SW p. 68.
- ☐ **{Optional} Lapbooking Templates** – Have the students complete the Oxidation and Reduction wheel-book on LT p. 41. Have them cut along the solid lines, punch a hole in the center, and use a brad fastener to fasten the two circles together. Have the students write several sentences about what they have learned about oxidation and reduction reactions. Finally, have them glue their mini-book into the lapbook.
- ☐ **{Optional} Coloring Pages** – Have the students color the following pages: Combustion CP p. 36, Photosynthesis CP p. 37.

Vocabulary
Have the students look up and copy the definition for the following word:
- **Redox Reaction** – A chemical reaction that involves the transfer of electrons. (SW p. 116)

{Optional} Weekly Review Sheet
- "Chemical Changes Weekly Review Sheet 4" on SW p. 158.

   Answers:
   1. True
   2. Oxidation
   3. Reduction
   4. Answers will vary

134

Chemistry for the Grammar Stage

Mixtures Unit

Mixtures Unit Overview
(4 weeks)

Books Scheduled
📖 *Usborne Science Encyclopedia*

{Optional Encyclopedias}
📖 *Basher Science Chemistry*
📖 *DK Children's Encyclopedia*

Sequence for Study
- **Week 1:** Mixtures
- **Week 2:** Separating Mixtures
- **Week 3:** Crystals
- **Week 4:** Scientist Study - Louis Pasteur

Mixtures Poem to Memorize

<u>Mixtures, Solutions, Oh My!</u>
A mixture occurs when two things combine
Like in air, Kool-Aid, and a salty brine

A solid and liquid together mix
And form a solution—a mixture trick

One separates a mixture many ways
Filter, distill, evaporate—some stays

Through chromatography, people can see
Ink separate into colors with glee

Supplies Needed for the Unit

Week	Supplies needed
1	Clear glass, Warm water, Powdered sugar
2	Washable markers, Coffee filter, Shallow dish or pan
3	Glass jar, Pencil, Pipe cleaners, Borax, Hot water
4	*No supplies needed.*

Unit Vocabulary
1. **Mixture** – A combination of two or more elements that are not chemically bonded together.
2. **Solution** – A mixture that consists of a substance dissolved in a liquid.
3. **Chromatography** – A method of separating the substances in a mixture by the rate they move through or along a medium, such as filter paper.
4. **Crystal** – A solid substance with a definite geometrical shape, straight edges, and flat surfaces; hard, glassy-looking objects made of minerals.

Week 1: Mixtures Lesson Plans

2-Days-a-week Schedule		
	Day 1	**Day 2**
Read	☐ Read "Mixtures, Part 1" ☐ {Choose one or more of the additional resources to read from this week}	☐ Read "Mixtures, Part 2" ☐ {Work on memorizing the "Mixtures, Solutions, Oh My!" poem}
Do	☐ {Make a Frozen Mixture or Work on the Mixtures Poster}	☐ Do the Scientific Demonstration: Disappearing Powder
Write	☐ Add information about mixtures to the students' notebook or lapbook ☐ Define mixture and solution	☐ Add information about mixtures to the students' notebook or lapbook ☐ Complete the demonstration sheet ☐ {Work on the Mixtures Weekly Review Sheet 1}

5-Days-a-week Schedule					
	Day 1	**Day 2**	**Day 3**	**Day 4**	**Day 5**
Read	☐ Read "Mixtures, Part 1"	☐ Read "Mixtures, Part 2"	☐ {Work on memorizing the "Mixtures, Solutions, Oh My!" poem}	☐ {Choose one or more of the additional resources to read from this week}	☐ {Choose one or more of the additional resources to read from this week}
Do	☐ {Make a Frozen Mixture}	☐ {Create a Liquid Mixture}	☐ Do the Scientific Demonstration: Disappearing Powder	☐ {Work on the Mixtures Poster}	
Write	☐ Add information about mixtures to the students' notebook or lapbook	☐ Add information about mixtures to the students' notebook or lapbook	☐ Complete the demonstration sheet	☐ Define mixture and solution	☐ {Work on the Mixtures Weekly Review Sheet 1}

{These assignments are optional.}

Read – Information Gathering

Reading Assignments

❑ *Usborne Science Encyclopedia* p. 58 "Mixtures, Part 1"
  ? What is a mixture?
  ? Can you tell me some examples of mixtures?
  ? What is a solute? A solvent?

❑ *Usborne Science Encyclopedia* p. 59 "Mixtures, Part 2"
  ? What does it mean when two liquids are miscible? Immiscible?
  ? Do you remember what an emulsion is?

{Optional} Memory Work

🗣 This week, begin memorizing the *Mixtures, Solutions, Oh My!* poem. (SW p. 124)

{Optional} Additional Resources

Encyclopedias
📖 *Basher Science Chemistry* p. 21 "Mixture"

Library Books
📖 *Compounds and Mixtures (Explorer Library: Science Explorer)* by Charnan Simon
📖 *Mixtures and Solutions (Why Chemistry Matters)* by Molly Aloian
📖 *Mix It Up! Solution or Mixture?* by Tracy Nelson Maurer
📖 *Mixtures and Solutions (Building Blocks of Matter)* by Richard Spilsbury and Louise Spilsbury

Do – Demonstration and Activities

Demonstration – Disappearing Powder

You will need the following:
- ✓ Clear glass
- ✓ Warm water
- ✓ Powdered sugar

Demonstration Instructions

1. Read the following introduction to the students.

    In this unit, we are going to learn about mixtures and solutions. Air is a mixture of gases. Seawater is a mixture of water and salts. Soil is a mixture of different solids. In this demonstration, we are going to see what happens when we make a mixture of powdered sugar and water!

2. Fill the glass about halfway with warm water.
3. Have the students take a pinch of powdered sugar and sprinkle it into the water. Have them

observe what happens. (**Note—**If the sugar doesn't dissolve all the way, you can stir it a bit until it does dissolve.)

4. Have the students repeat the process, adding another pinch of powdered sugar.
5. Read the demonstration explanation to the students and have them complete the demonstration sheet on SW p. 75.

Demonstration Explanation

The purpose of this demonstration was for the students to see the formation of a solution. When they are done, read the following to them:

> When you sprinkled the powdered sugar into the water it disappeared. This is called dissolving. The water breaks the pieces of sugar into smaller and smaller bits. Then those bits spread out evenly throughout the water, creating a special mixture called a solution.

{Optional} Take the Demonstration Further

Have the students test different types of powders from your home. For example, things like salt and baking soda will dissolve, whereas cornstarch and sand will not.

{Optional} Unit Project

✂ **Mixtures Poster –** Over the course of this unit, the students will make a poster showing what they have learned about mixtures. This week, have them write the definition of a mixture and add several pictures and names of mixtures they can find in their homes. (*This has been done for you in the SW on p. 72.*)

{Optional} Projects for This Week

✂ **Frozen Mixture –** Have the students make a frozen solution - ice cream in a bag! You will need ½ cup of heavy cream, ½ cup of milk, 1 tablespoon of sugar, ½ teaspoon of vanilla, 1 quart-size ziploc plastic bag, 2 cups of crushed ice, 1 gallon-size ziploc plastic bag, and ½ cup of rock salt. Begin by adding the cream, milk, sugar, and vanilla to the quart-size bag, close it, and shake vigorously to mix well. Then, add the ice and rock salt to the gallon-size bag, mix well, and then nestle the quart-size bag into the ice mixture. Seal the large baggie up tightly and begin shaking! (**Note—***It will take about 10 to 15 minutes for ice cream to form. You can use a towel or oven mitt to hold the large baggie as you shake if it gets too cold to handle.*)

✂ **Liquid Mixture –** Have the students make an emulsion. You will need a water bottle, water, and oil. Pour about a cup of water into the bottle and a cup of oil. Then, seal the bottle tightly and observe how the two liquids remain separated. Now, have the students shake the bottle vigorously for one minute. Have them observe the emulsion that was created.

Write – Notebooking
Writing Assignments
- ☐ **Student Workbook** – Have the students dictate, copy, or write two to four sentences on mixtures on SW p. 74.
- ☐ **{Optional} Lapbooking Templates** – Have the students begin the Mixtures lapbook by cutting out and coloring the cover on LT p. 43.
- ☐ **{Optional} Lapbooking Templates** – Have the students complete the Mixtures Mini-book on LT p. 44. Have them cut out and fold the templates. Have the students color the cover. Then, have the students write a sentence or two about mixtures on the inside. Finally, glue the mini-book into the lapbook.
- ☐ **{Optional} Coloring Pages** – Have the students color the following page: Mixtures CP p. 38.

Vocabulary
Have the students look up and copy the definitions for the following words:
- **Mixture** – A combination of two or more elements that are not chemically bonded together. (SW p. 113)
- **Solution** – A mixture that consists of a substance dissolved in a liquid. (SW p. 117)

{Optional} Weekly Review Sheet
- "Mixtures Weekly Review Sheet 1" on SW p. 159.

    Answers:
    1. True
    2. Solid
    3. Miscible, Immiscible
    4. Answers will vary

Week 2: Separating Mixtures Lesson Plans

2-Days-a-week Schedule		
	Day 1	Day 2
Read	❏ Read "Separating Mixtures, Part 1" ❏ {Choose one or more of the additional resources to read from this week}	❏ Read "Separating Mixtures, Part 2" ❏ {Work on memorizing the "Mixtures, Solutions, Oh My!" poem}
Do	❏ {Filter some dirty water or Work on the Mixtures Poster}	❏ Do the Scientific Demonstration: Separating Colors
Write	❏ Add information about separating mixtures to the students' notebook or lapbook ❏ Define chromatography	❏ Add information about separating mixtures to the students' notebook or lapbook ❏ Complete the demonstration sheet ❏ {Work on the Mixtures Weekly Review Sheet 2}

5-Days-a-week Schedule					
	Day 1	Day 2	Day 3	Day 4	Day 5
Read	❏ Read "Separating Mixtures, Part 1"	❏ Read "Separating Mixtures, Part 2"	❏ {Work on memorizing the "Mixtures, Solutions, Oh My!" poem}	❏ {Choose one or more of the additional resources to read from this week}	❏ {Choose one or more of the additional resources to read from this week}
Do	❏ {Filter some dirty water}	❏ {Watch a video on distillation}	❏ Do the Scientific Demonstration: Separating Colors	❏ {Work on the Mixtures Poster}	
Write	❏ Add information about separating mixtures to the students' notebook or lapbook	❏ Add information about separating mixtures to the students' notebook or lapbook	❏ Complete the demonstration sheet	❏ Define chromatography	❏ {Work on the Mixtures Weekly Review Sheet 2}

Read - Information Gathering

Reading Assignments

- ❑ *Usborne Science Encyclopedia* p. 60 "Separating Mixtures, Part 1"
    - **?** What is decantation?
    - **?** Do you remember what filtration is used to separate?
    - **?** Do you remember what chromatography is used to separate?
- ❑ *Usborne Science Encyclopedia* p. 61 "Separating Mixtures, Part 2"
    - **?** What is evaporation?
    - **?** Do you remember what happens during distillation?
    - **?** What is centrifuging?

{Optional} Memory Work
- This week, begin memorizing the *Mixtures, Solutions, Oh My!* poem. (SW p. 124)

{Optional} Additional Resources
Encyclopedias
- 📖 *Basher Science Chemistry* p. 62 "Filter," p. 63 "Distillation", p. 66 "Chromatography"
- 📖 *DK Children's Encyclopedia* p. 195 "Mixtures"

Library Books
- 📖 *Mixing and Separating (Changing Materials)* by Chris Oxlade
- 📖 *Mixtures and Compounds (Internet-linked Library of Science)* by Alastair Smith and P. Clarke

Do - Demonstration and Activities

Demonstration - Separating Colors
You will need the following:
- ✓ Washable markers
- ✓ Coffee filter
- ✓ Shallow dish or pan

Demonstration Instructions
1. Read the following introduction to the students.

    Last week, we learned about mixtures. This week, we are going to study several ways to separate those mixtures. Did you know that certain markers are a mixture of colors? In this demonstration, we are going to use water to see those different colors.

2. Have the students fold the coffee filter in half and then fold it in half again so that it is in the shape of a piece of pie. Then, have them draw a thick line of color with the marker on the

long edge of the coffee filter about half an inch above the edge.
3. Meanwhile, cover the bottom of the dish or pan with a thin layer of water. Have the students gently set the long edge of the filter in the water so that the paper touches the water, but not the marker lines.
4. Allow the filter to sit in the water undisturbed for 30 minutes. Then, have the students observe the changes in the marker lines.
5. Read the demonstration explanation to the students and have them complete the demonstration sheet on SW p. 77.

Demonstration Explanation

The purpose of this demonstration was for the students to see how the different colors in ink can be separated out. When they are done, read the following to them:

> We saw that as the water spread out, it picks up part of the ink - creating a trail of ink. Some washable markers are made up of several different types of ink, all of which are soluble in water. The water picks up the molecules of ink and carries them along the filter paper. Some of these ink molecules are heavier than the others. So, the water separates the ink into different colors by depositing the heavier molecules sooner than the lighter ones.

{Optional} Take the Demonstration Further

Have the students use chromatography and markers to make some tie-dye art! The directions for this activity can be found here:
- https://elementalscience.com/blogs/science-activities/marker-chromatography-steam-activity

{Optional} Unit Project

- **Mixtures Poster** – Have the students add a bit about the three methods for separating mixtures that they learned this week to the middle of their posters.

{Optional} Projects for This Week

- **Filtration** – Have the students filter some dirty water. You will need dirty water, a funnel, a jar, a coffee filter, plus some sand and gravel. (**Note**-*You can easily make dirty water by adding some dirt, twigs, and/or leaves.*) Have the students set the funnel in the mouth of the jar and line it with the coffee filter, add a bit of sand, and then top it off with gravel. Next, have the students slowly pour the dirty water into their filter and watch what happens.
- **Distillation** – Have the students watch the following video on separating a mixture of salt and water through distillation:
  - https://www.youtube.com/watch?v=N0f73tbGCRE

Write – Notebooking

Writing Assignments

- ☐ **Student Workbook** – Have the students dictate, copy, or write two to four sentences on separating mixtures on SW p. 76.
- ☐ **{Optional} Lapbooking Templates** – Have the students complete the Separating Mixtures Flap-book on LT pp. 45-46. Have the students cut out the sheets. Have them color the pictures on each sheet. Then, have the students write several sentences about what they have learned on the filtration, chromatography, and distillation sheets. Finally, glue the mini-book into the lapbook.
- ☐ **{Optional} Coloring Pages** – Have the students color the following pages: Filtration CP p. 39, Chromatography CP p. 40, and Distillation CP p. 41.

Vocabulary

Have the students look up and copy the definition for the following word:

- **Chromatography** – A method of separating the substances in a mixture by the rate they move through or along a medium, such as filter paper. (SW p. 108)

{Optional} Weekly Review Sheet

- "Mixtures Weekly Review Sheet 2" on SW p. 160.

    Answers:
    1. Solids from liquids
    2. False (*Chromatography is an excellent way to separate the colors in ink.*)
    3. Liquids
    4. Answers will vary

Week 3: Crystals Lesson Plans

2-Days-a-week Schedule		
	Day 1	**Day 2**
Read	❏ Read "Crystals, Part 1" ❏ {Choose one or more of the additional resources to read from this week}	❏ Read "Crystals, Part 2" ❏ {Work on memorizing the "Mixtures, Solutions, Oh My!" poem}
Do	❏ {Go on a crystal hunt or Work on the Mixtures Poster}	❏ Do the Scientific Demonstration: Crystalline Shapes
Write	❏ Add information about crystals to the students' notebook or lapbook ❏ Define crystal	❏ Add information about crystals to the students' notebook or lapbook ❏ Complete the demonstration sheet ❏ {Work on the Mixtures Weekly Review Sheet 3}

5-Days-a-week Schedule					
	Day 1	**Day 2**	**Day 3**	**Day 4**	**Day 5**
Read	❏ Read "Crystals, Part 1"	❏ Read "Crystals, Part 2"	❏ {Work on memorizing the "Mixtures, Solutions, Oh My!" poem}	❏ {Choose one or more of the additional resources to read from this week}	❏ {Choose one or more of the additional resources to read from this week}
Do	❏ {Go on a crystal hunt}	❏ {Make sugar crystals}	❏ Do the Scientific Demonstration: Crystalline Shapes		❏ {Work on the Mixtures Poster}
Write	❏ Add information about crystals to the students' notebook or lapbook	❏ Add information about crystals to the students' notebook or lapbook	❏ Complete the demonstration sheet	❏ Define crystal	❏ {Work on the Mixtures Weekly Review Sheet 3}

Read – Information Gathering

Reading Assignments

- ❑ *Usborne Science Encyclopedia* p. 90 "Crystals, Part 1"
  - **?** What are crystals?
  - **?** Do you remember how do crystals form?
  - **?** Can you tell me how we use crystals every day?

- ❑ *Usborne Science Encyclopedia* p. 91 "Crystals, Part 2"
  - **?** Do you remember what it means to be hydrated?
  - **?** What kinds of crystals can we find in the earth's crust?

{Optional} Memory Work

- 🗣 This week, begin memorizing the *Mixtures, Solutions, Oh My!* poem. (SW p. 124)

{Optional} Additional Resources

Encyclopedias
- 📖 *There are no optional pages for this topic.*

Library Books
- 📖 *Crystals (Rocks and Minerals)* by Connor Dayton
- 📖 *Growing Crystals* by Ann O Squire
- 📖 *What Are Crystals? (Let's Rock!)* by Molly Aloian
- 📖 *DK Eyewitness Books: Crystal & Gem* by R.F. Symes

Do – Demonstration and Activities

Demonstration – Crystalline Shapes

You will need the following:
- ✓ Glass jar
- ✓ Pencil
- ✓ Pipe cleaners
- ✓ Borax (**Note–***You will need about a quarter to a half of a cup of Borax for this demonstration. You can find Borax in the laundry aisle of the local grocery store - be sure to buy the one labeled laundry booster, not the soap that includes Borax.*)
- ✓ Hot water

Demonstration Instructions

1. Read the following introduction to the students.

   Last week, we talked about separating mixtures. One of the ways we can do this is by crystallization, which is what we are studying this week. This method is best to use with a solid liquid mixture. For example we could use crystallization to separate a mixture of water and Borax cystals, which is exactly what we are going to do in this week's demonstration.

2. Have the students shape the pipe cleaners into their desired shapes. (**Note**–*This can be as simple or as complex as they wish, but make sure it will fit through the opening of their jar.*)
3. Next, attach the shape to the pencil using another pipe cleaner. (**Note**–*You want the pencil to be able to rest on the edge of the jar without having the shape touch the sides or bottom of the jar.*)
4. Now, add hot water until it almost fills the jar, noting how many cups of water it takes to fill the jar.
5. Then, add the Borax, one tablespoon at a time, taking care each time to stir until the Borax is dissolved. (**Note**–*You want to add about three tablespoons of Borax for every cup of water added.*)
6. Finally, hang the shape in the jar so that it is completely covered by the liquid and allow the jar to sit undisturbed overnight.
7. The next morning, have the students observe what happens. Then, read the demonstration explanation to the students and have them complete the demonstration sheet on SW p. 79.

Demonstration Explanation

The purpose of this demonstration was for the students to see the formation of crystals.. When they are done, read the following to them:

> After the mixture sat overnight, the crystals we added to the water came back out. Only this time, they were bigger, and they attached themselves to the pipe cleaners and the jar! The structure of these crystals is the same as the smaller version that we added to the water. So this gives us a chance to observe that structure up close.

{Optional} Take the Demonstration Further

Have the students make alum crystals. The directions for this project can be found in the "See for yourself" box on p. 91 of the *Usborne Science Encyclopedia*.

{Optional} Unit Project

✂ **Mixtures Poster** – Have the students add the definition of a crystal to the bottom third of their poster. Then, have them go on a crystal hunt to find crystals. Have the students take, cut out, or draw pictures of the crystals they find and add those to their poster.

{Optional} Projects for This Week

✂ **Crystal Hunt** – Have the students search the house for crystals. They can look for examples in jewelry, in rock collections, and in the kitchen! The students can use the examples they have found on their mixtures poster.

✂ **Sugar Crystals** – Have the students make sugar crystals. You will need 3 cups of sugar, 1 cup of water, a jar, a pencil, string, foil, and a pot. Have the students tie the string to the pencil, so that it hangs just above the bottom of the jar. In the pot, mix the sugar and water and heat until the sugar is dissolved. Let the mixture cool a bit before pouring it into the jar.

Cover with foil and set the jar in a place where it won't be disturbed for several weeks. Have the students observe the jar each day. When the crystals are big enough, usually about one to two weeks later, you can take them out, eat, and enjoy!

Write - Notebooking

Writing Assignments
- **Student Workbook** – Have the students dictate, copy, or write two to four sentences on crystals on SW p. 78.
- **{Optional} Lapbooking Templates** – Have the students complete the Crystals Hexa-book on LT p. 47. Have the students cut out the template. Have the students write several sentences about what they have learned about crystals. Then, have them glue the mini-book into the lapbook.
- **{Optional} Coloring Pages** – Have the students color the following pages: Crystals CP p. 42.

Vocabulary
Have the students look up and copy the definition for the following word:
- **Crystal** – A solid substance with a definite geometrical shape, straight edges, and flat surfaces. (SW p. 108)

{Optional} Weekly Review Sheet
- "Mixtures Weekly Review Sheet 3" on SW p. 161.
    Answers:
    1. Cools off
    2. True
    3. False (*Crystals have straight edges and flat surfaces.*)
    4. Answers will vary

Week 4: Scientist Biography Lesson Plans

2-Days-a-week Schedule		
	Day 1	Day 2
Read	❑ Read *Germ Hunter: A Story about Louis Pasteur* Chapters 1-3 ❑ {Work on memorizing the "Mixtures, Solutions, Oh My!" poem}	❑ Read *Germ Hunter: A Story about Louis Pasteur* Chapters 4-6
Write	❑ Add information about the scientist to the students' Scientist Biography Report Sheet	❑ Add information about the scientist to the students' Scientist Biography Report Sheet ❑ {Work on the Mixtures Weekly Review Sheet 4}

5-Days-a-week Schedule					
	Day 1	Day 2	Day 3	Day 4	Day 5
Read	❑ Read *Germ Hunter: A Story about Louis Pasteur* Chapters 1	❑ Read *Germ Hunter: A Story about Louis Pasteur* Chapters 2-3	❑ Read *Germ Hunter: A Story about Louis Pasteur* Chapters 4-5	❑ Read *Germ Hunter: A Story about Louis Pasteur* Chapters 6	❑ {Work on memorizing the "Mixtures, Solutions, Oh My!" poem}
Write	❑ Add information about the scientist to the students' Scientist Biography Report Sheet	❑ Add information about the scientist to the students' Scientist Biography Report Sheet	❑ Add information about the scientist to the students' Scientist Biography Report Sheet	❑ Add information about the scientist to the students' Scientist Biography Report Sheet	❑ {Write a written report on the scientist} ❑ {Work on the Mixtures Weekly Review Sheet 4}

Read – Information Gathering

Reading Assignment

During this week, the students will read a biography on Louis Pasteur, a famous scientists who made many discoveries in the field of chemistry, including pasteurization. You can purchase the recommended book below, or you can get another book from the library. You can read the book out loud to your students or have them read it on their own. I have included a possible schedule for you with this week's materials.

 📖 *Germ Hunter: A Story about Louis Pasteur* by Elaine Marie Alphin

As you read, have the students tell you what they have learned about Mr. Pasteur. You can ask the following questions:

- **?** Who was the scientist you read about?
- **?** When and where was he born?
- **?** What was his major scientific contribution?
- **?** List the events that surround his discovery.
- **?** List some other interesting events in the scientist's life.
- **?** Why do you think that it is important to learn about this scientist?

{Optional} Memory Work

- This week, finish memorizing the "Mixtures, Solutions, Oh My!" poem. (SW p. 124)

Write – Notebooking

Writing Assignments

- ☐ **Student Workbook –** Have the students fill out the Scientist Biography Report Sheet on SW pp. 80-81.

{Optional} Scientist Biography Report

Once you have completed the book, you can also have the students write a full report on Louis Pasteur. Have them write a rough draft using their responses on the Scientist Biography Report Sheet. It should include the following:

- ✓ An introductory paragraph
- ✓ A paragraph on Pasteur's scientific contributions
- ✓ A paragraph on other interesting events in the scientist's life
- ✓ A conclusion that includes why the students feel it is important to study this particular scientist

After they complete the rough draft, have them proofread and correct mistakes. Finally, have them give their report a title and rewrite it as a final draft. If you want to make the final report a

little more interesting, here are two options:
1. Have the students turn their report into a mini-book on the scientist, including pictures they have drawn.
2. Have the students make a poster to present their report.

{Optional} Weekly Review Sheet
✦ "Mixture Unit Week 4 Quiz" on SW p. 162.
   Answers:
   1. Answers will vary.

Chemistry for the Grammar Stage

Acids and Bases Unit

Acids and Bases Unit Overview
(4 weeks)

Books Scheduled
📖 *Usborne Science Encyclopedia*

{Optional Encyclopedias}
📖 *Basher Science Chemistry*
📖 *Usborne Children's Encyclopedia*
📖 *DK Children's Encyclopedia*

Neutral

Base

Acid

Sequence for Study
- Week 1: Acids and Bases
- Week 2: pH
- Week 3: Neutralization
- Week 4: Scientist Study - Marie Curie

Unit Prep Note
For this unit, there are two supplies, cabbage indicator and cabbage paper, both of which you will need to make up ahead of time. The directions for making cabbage indicator are as follows:

Supplies Needed
- ✓ Head of purple cabbage
- ✓ Knife
- ✓ Pot
- ✓ Distilled water
- ✓ Strainer
- ✓ Clear glass jar or plastic container
- ✓ Coffee Filters
- ✓ Bowl
- ✓ Cookie Sheet
- ✓ Scissors
- ✓ Plastic baggie

How to Make Cabbage Indicator
1. Chop up about a half of the purple cabbage head. Place it in the pot and cover it with water.
2. Bring the water to a boil and let it boil for 10 to 15 minutes – basically until the water is a deep purple color.
3. Let cool the cabbage juice before straining about two cups of the liquid into the clear glass jar or plastic container.

How to Make Cabbage Paper
1. Strain the remaining cabbage juice into a bowl. (*This should be at least a cup.*)
2. Dip a coffee filter into the cabbage juice, soaking it completely. Then, take it out and set it on the cookie sheet to dry. Repeat this with at lease two more coffee filters.
3. When the filters are dry, cut them into strips and store them in a plastic baggie.

Acids and Bases Poem to Memorize

Acids and Bases

Acids dissolve in water to taste sour
Like the vinegar next to your flour

Bases break up into bitter compounds
Which can clean up stains left by coffee grounds

We measure their strength by the pH scale
Low for acids, high for base, tells the tale

But when we mix an acid and a base
Now, neutralization is what takes place

We see water and salt are left behind
A pH of 7 is what we find

Supplies Needed for the Unit

Week	Supplies needed
Unit Prep*	Head of purple cabbage, Knife, Pot, Distilled water, Strainer, Clear glass jar or plastic container, Coffee Filters, Bowl, Cookie Sheet, Scissors, Plastic baggie
1	Water, Lemon juice, Cabbage indicator, Glass, Tablespoon
2	Cabbage paper, Vinegar, Ammonia, Jars with lids
3	Vinegar, Baking soda, Water, Cabbage juice, Cabbage paper, 2 Clear cups, Eyedropper
4	*No supplies needed.*

Unit Vocabulary

1. **Acid** – A chemical that dissolves in water and can neutralize a base. Weak acids taste sour.
2. **Base** – A chemical that dissolves in water and can neutralize an acid. Weak bases taste bitter.
3. **Indicator** – A substance that changes color in the presence of an acid or base.
4. **pH** – A scale from 0 to 14 used to measure the strength of acids and bases.
5. **Neutralization** – A reaction where one substance fully or partly cancels out another.
6. **Salt** – An ionic compound that when dissolved in water makes positive and negative ions. A salt is produced when you combine an acid and a base.

Week 1: Acids and Bases Lesson Plans

2-Days-a-week Schedule		
	Day 1	**Day 2**
Read	☐ Read "Acids and Bases, Part 1" ☐ *{Choose one or more of the additional resources to read from this week}*	☐ Read "Acids and Bases, Part 2" ☐ *{Work on memorizing the "Acids and Bases" poem}*
Do	☐ *{Do the Acid Base Reaction or Work on the Mixtures Poster}*	☐ Do the Scientific Demonstration: Kitchen Acid
Write	☐ Add information about acids to the students' notebook or lapbook ☐ Define acid and base	☐ Add information about bases to the students' notebook or lapbook ☐ Complete the demonstration sheet ☐ *{Work on the Acids and Bases Weekly Review Sheet 1}*

5-Days-a-week Schedule					
	Day 1	**Day 2**	**Day 3**	**Day 4**	**Day 5**
Read	☐ Read "Acids and Bases, Part 1"	☐ Read "Acids and Bases, Part 2"	☐ *{Work on memorizing the "Acids and Bases" poem}*	☐ *{Choose one or more of the additional resources to read from this week}*	☐ *{Choose one or more of the additional resources to read from this week}*
Do	☐ *{Work on the Acids and Bases Poster}*	☐ *{Do the Acid Base Reaction}*	☐ Do the Scientific Demonstration: Kitchen Acid	☐ *{Do the Neutralization activity}*	
Write	☐ Add information about acids to the students' notebook or lapbook	☐ Add information about bases to the students' notebook or lapbook	☐ Complete the demonstration sheet	☐ Define acid and base	☐ *{Work on the Acids and Bases Weekly Review Sheet 1}*

{These assignments are optional.}

Read – Information Gathering

Reading Assignments
- ❑ *Usborne Science Encyclopedia* p. 84 "Acids and Bases, Part 1"
    - ? What is an acid?
    - ? What is the difference between a strong and a weak acid?
    - ? Do you remember some of the common acids?
- ❑ *Usborne Science Encyclopedia* p. 85 "Acids and Bases, Part 2"
    - ? What is a base?
    - ? What is the difference between a strong and a weak base?
    - ? Do you remember some of the common bases?

{Optional} Memory Work
- This week, begin memorizing the *Acids and Bases* poem. (SW p. 125)

{Optional} Additional Resources
Encyclopedias
- *Basher Science Chemistry* p. 46 "Acid," p. 48 "Bases"

Library Books
- *Acids and Bases (Why Chemistry Matters)* by Lynnette Brent
- *Acids & Bases (Material Matters)* by Carol Baldwin
- *Acids and Bases (Chemicals in Action)* by Chris Oxlade

Do – Demonstration and Activities

Demonstration – Kitchen Acid
You will need the following:
- ✓ Water
- ✓ Lemon juice
- ✓ Cabbage indicator (*See the unit prep note on p. 154.*)
- ✓ Glass
- ✓ Tablespoon

Demonstration Instructions
1. Read the following introduction to the students.

    In this unit, we are going to learn about two special kinds of chemicals, acids and bases. The two groups of chemicals are opposites of each other and can react in spectacular ways. We see them frequently in our daily lives. Acids are responsible for the sourness of a grapefruit and bases can be found in toothpaste that helps clean our teeth. In this demonstration, we are going to use a special liquid, called an indicator, to see if an acid is present.

2. Add 2 tablespoons of the cabbage juice to a cup. Ask the students to note the color of the liquid on the chart on the demonstration sheet on SW p. 87. Explain how the cabbage juice can change color using the following:

> Cabbage juice by itself is a bluish-purple color. When we add an acid, it turns purple or pink, depending on the strength of the acid. When we add a base, it turns blue or green, depending on the strength of the base. This is why cabbage juice is called an indicator solution.

3. Next, add 2 tablespoons of water to the cup and mix well. Ask the students to note the color of the liquid on the chart on the demonstration sheet.
4. Then, add 2 tablespoons of lemon juice to the cup and mix well. Ask the students to note the color of the liquid on the chart on the demonstration sheet.
5. Read the demonstration explanation to the students and have them complete the demonstration sheet.

Demonstration Explanation

The purpose of this demonstration was for the students to see help the students see that acids can be found in their kitchens. When they are done, read the following to them:

> We saw that the cabbage juice by itself was a bluish-purple color, which is its color in a neutral solution. When we added water, the color didn't really change. This is because water is also neutral. But, when we added the lemon juice, we saw a big change! The liquid turned bright purple and pink. This is because lemon juice is an acid. The cabbage juice indicated this for us, which is why it is such a great indicator solution.

{Optional} Take the Demonstration Further

Have the students test other drinks in your refrigerator using the same process you used in the demonstration.

{Optional} Unit Project

✂ **Acids and Bases Poster** – Over this unit, the students will create two posters with the acids and bases they encounter. For example, this week, they could add lemonade to the acid poster and baking soda to the base poster. They can simply write the names or they can use pictures. (*This has been done for you in the SW on pp. 84-85.*)

{Optional} Projects for This Week

✂ **Acid Base Reaction** – Have the students see what happens when you mix an acid and a base. You will need baking soda, vinegar and a glass. The directions for this activity can be found in the *Usborne Science Encyclopedia* on p. 85.

✂ **Neutralization** – Have the students neutralize an acid with a base. You will need vinegar, cabbage juice, baking soda, and a clear glass. Pour about a quarter of a cup of vinegar into the glass and set it in the sink. Have the students add about a teaspoon of the cabbage juice, which should turn the solution a pinkish color. Then, add a tablespoon of baking soda and watch what happens! (*Similar to the previous activity, there should be a strong, bubbling reaction that eventually calms down. The difference is that this time, the color of the solution should change to a neutral bluish-purple color.*)

Write - Notebooking

Writing Assignments
- **Student Workbook** – Have the students dictate, copy, or write two to four sentences on acids and bases on SW p. 86.
- **{Optional} Lapbooking Templates** – Have the students complete the Acids and Bases tab-book on LT p. 48. Have them cut out and color the pictures on the cover. Then, have the students write what they have learned about acids and bases on their respective tabs. Have them staple the mini-book together and glue it into the lapbook.
- **{Optional} Coloring Pages** – Have the students color the following pages: Acids CP p. 43, Bases CP p. 44.

Vocabulary
Have the students look up and copy the definitions for the following words:
- **Acid** – A chemical that dissolves in water and can neutralize a base. Weak acids taste sour. (SW p. 106)
- **Base** – A chemical that dissolves in water and can neutralize an acid. Weak bases taste bitter. (SW p. 107)

{Optional} Weekly Review Sheet
- "Acids and Bases Weekly Review Sheet 1" on SW p. 163.
    Answers:
    1. True
    2. Vinegar, Lemon juice
    3. False (*A base dissolves in water and can taste bitter.*)
    4. Baking soda, Ammonia
    5. Answers will vary

Week 2: pH Lesson Plans

2-Days-a-week Schedule		
	Day 1	**Day 2**
Read	❑ Read "Acids and Bases, Part 3" ❑ {Choose one or more of the additional resources to read from this week}	❑ Read "Acids and Bases, Part 4" ❑ {Work on memorizing the "Acids and Bases" poem}
Do	❑ {Create your own pH scale or Work on the Mixtures Poster}	❑ Do the Scientific Demonstration: Testing Strips
Write	❑ Add information about acids and bases to the students' notebook or lapbook ❑ Define indicator and pH	❑ Add information about acids and bases to the students' notebook or lapbook ❑ Complete the demonstration sheet ❑ {Work on the Acids and Bases Weekly Review Sheet 2}

5-Days-a-week Schedule					
	Day 1	**Day 2**	**Day 3**	**Day 4**	**Day 5**
Read	❑ Read "Acids and Bases, Part 3"	❑ Read "Acids and Bases, Part 4"	❑ {Work on memorizing the "Acids and Bases" poem}	❑ {Choose one or more of the additional resources to read from this week}	❑ {Choose one or more of the additional resources to read from this week}
Do	❑ {Create your own pH scale}	❑ {Try another indicator}	❑ Do the Scientific Demonstration: Testing Strips	❑ {Work on the Acids and Bases Poster}	
Write	❑ Add information about acids and bases to the students' notebook or lapbook	❑ Add information about acids and bases to the students' notebook or lapbook	❑ Complete the demonstration sheet	❑ Define indicator and pH	❑ {Work on the Acids and Bases Weekly Review Sheet 2}

Read – Information Gathering

Reading Assignments
- ❑ *Usborne Science Encyclopedia* p. 86 "Acids and Bases, Part 3"
    - ? Can you tell me what pH stands for?
    - ? What does a low pH, under 7, stand for? A pH of 7? A high pH, over 7?
    - ? Do you remember what an indicator does?
- ❑ *Usborne Science Encyclopedia* p. 87 "Acids and Bases, Part 4"
    - ? What do you remember about sulfuric acid?

{Optional} Memory Work
- 🗣 This week, begin memorizing the *Acids and Bases* poem. (SW p. 125)

{Optional} Additional Resources
Encyclopedias
- 📖 *Basher Science Chemistry* p. 50 "pH," p. 52 "Indicator"

Library Books
There are no additional books on the market for these topics. Instead, you can watch the following videos on pH:
- 🖱 Importance of pH in everyday life: https://www.youtube.com/watch?v=x-nI3Ws7nxQ
- 🖱 What is the pH scale? https://www.youtube.com/watch?v=3U9n4BV2618

Do – Demonstration and Activities

Demonstration – Testing Strips
You will need the following:
- ✓ Cabbage paper (*See the unit prep note on p. 154.*)
- ✓ Vinegar
- ✓ Ammonia
- ✓ 2 Jars with lids

Demonstration Instructions
1. Read the following introduction to the students.

    Last week, we learned about acids and bases. Scientists use indicator solutions or pH paper to test how acidic or how basic a chemical is. In this demonstration, we are going to use cabbage paper, which can be used as pH paper, to test several chemicals in the kitchen.

2. Fill one jar halfway with vinegar and the other jar halfway with ammonia.
3. Have the students take a strip of cabbage paper and dip it into the jar with vinegar. Then, set the strip on the lid to dry.

4. Have them observe the color change and write it on the chart of the demonstration sheet on SW p. 89.
5. Have the students take a strip of cabbage paper and dip it into the jar with ammonica. Then, set the strip on the lid to dry.
6. Have them observe the color change and write it on the chart of the demonstration sheet.
7. Read the demonstration explanation to the students and have them complete the demonstration sheet.

Demonstration Explanation

The purpose of this demonstration was for the students to see test for the presence of an acid or a base. When they are done, read the following to them:

> When we dipped the cabbage paper in the jar with vinegar it turned pink. When we dipped the cabbage paper in the jar with ammonia it turned green. As we learned last week, cabbage juice can be used as an indicator. The cabbage paper was soaked in the cabbage juice, making it possible to use the paper as a type of pH paper.

{Optional} Take the Demonstration Further

Have the students use the paper to test several other liquids from the kitchen.

{Optional} Unit Project

- **Acids and Bases Poster** – This week, the students could add vinegar to the acid poster and ammonia to the base poster. They can simply write the names, or they can use pictures. The students can also add information about the pH scale (i.e., what range of the scale is considered an acid or a base) to their posters.

{Optional} Projects for This Week

- **pH** – Have the students create their own pH scale for the cabbage juice indicator. You can view one in the following post:
  - https://elementalscience.com/blogs/science-activities/kitchen-acid-test
- **Indicator** – Have the students use another indicator to test the acids and bases they know about so far. Grape juice is another option for an indicator. It turns reddish-purple in the presence of an acid and purplish-black in the presence of a base.

Write – Notebooking

Writing Assignments

- ☐ **Student Workbook** – Have the students dictate, copy, or write two to four sentences on pH and indicators on SW p. 88.
- ☐ **{Optional} Lapbooking Templates** – Have the students complete the pH Scale Sheet on LT p. 49. Have the students cut out and write whether the section is acidic, basic, or neutral.

Then, have the students color the acid range from dark (at 0) to light (before 7) red. Have them color the base section from dark (at 14) to light (before 7) blue. Have them leave the neutral section white. Finally, glue the sheet into the lapbook.

- {Optional} **Coloring Pages** – Have the students color the following pages: pH CP p. 45.

Vocabulary

Have the students look up and copy the definitions for the following words:
- **Indicator** – A substance that changes color in the presence of an acid or base. (SW p. 111)
- **pH** – A scale from 0 to 14 used to measure the strength of acids and bases. (SW p. 115)

{Optional} Weekly Review Sheet

- "Acids and Bases Weekly Review Sheet 2" on SW p. 164.

   Answers:
   1. Power of hydrogen
   2. pH 2 - acid, pH 7 - neutral, ph 10 - base
   3. True
   4. Answers will vary

Week 3: Neutralization Lesson Plans

	2-Days-a-week Schedule	
	Day 1	**Day 2**
Read	❏ Read "Neutralization" ❏ {Choose one or more of the additional resources to read from this week}	❏ Read "Salts" ❏ {Work on memorizing the "Acids and Bases" poem}
Do	❏ {Make some Fizzy Lemonade or Work on the Mixtures Poster}	❏ Do the Scientific Demonstration: Neutralize It
Write	❏ Add information about neutralization to the students' notebook or lapbook ❏ Define neutralization and salt	❏ Add information about salts to the students' notebook or lapbook ❏ Complete the demonstration sheet ❏ {Work on the Acids and Bases Weekly Review Sheet 3}

	5-Days-a-week Schedule				
	Day 1	**Day 2**	**Day 3**	**Day 4**	**Day 5**
Read	❏ Read "Neutralization"	❏ {Work on memorizing the "Acids and Bases" poem}	❏ Read "Salts, Part 1"	❏ Read "Salts, Part 2"	❏ {Choose one or more of the additional resources to read from this week}
Do	❏ {Make some Fizzy Lemonade}	❏ Do the Scientific Demonstration: Neutralize It	❏ {Do the Salt Creation Activity}	❏ {Work on the Acids and Bases Poster}	
Write	❏ Add information about neutralization to the students' notebook or lapbook	❏ Complete the demonstration sheet ❏ Define neutralization and salt	❏ Add information about salts to the students' notebook or lapbook	❏ Add information about salts to the students' notebook or lapbook	❏ {Work on the Acids and Bases Weekly Review Sheet 3}

Read – Information Gathering

Reading Assignments
- ☐ *"Neutralization"* article p. 168 of this guide
  - **?** What is neutralization?
  - **?** What happens when you mix an acid and a base?
- ☐ *Usborne Science Encyclopedia* pp. 89-90 "Salts"
  - **?** What is a salt?
  - **?** How can salts be formed?

{Optional} Memory Work
- This week, begin memorizing the *Acids and Bases* poem. (SW p. 125)

{Optional} Additional Resources
Encyclopedias
- 📖 *Basher Science Chemistry* p. 30 "Ions"

Library Books
- 📖 *From Sea to Salt (Start to Finish, Second Series)* by Lisa Owings
- 📖 *The Story of Salt* by Mark Kurlansky and S. D. Schindler

Do – Demonstration and Activities

Demonstration – Neutralize It
You will need the following:
- ✓ Vinegar
- ✓ Baking soda
- ✓ Water
- ✓ Cabbage juice
- ✓ Cabbage paper
- ✓ 2 Clear cups
- ✓ Eyedropper

Demonstration Instructions
1. Read the following introduction to the students.

   We have learned about acids and bases, plus how to use an indicator paper to test for them. Acids and bases can react together to neutralize one another. In this demonstration, we are going to mix an acid and a base until the pH is neutral.

2. Pour about a quarter of a cup of vinegar in the glass and set it in the sink. Dip a strip of your cabbage paper into the vinegar to test to see if it is an acid. (*It should turn a pinkish color, indicating the presence of an acid.*)

3. In another cup, mix 1 tablespoon of baking soda with a half of a cup of warm water. Stir until dissolved. Dip a strip of your cabbage paper into the vinegar to test to see if it is an

base. (*It should turn a bluish color, indicating the presence of a base.*)
4. Have the students add about a teaspoon of the cabbage juice to the cup in the sink, which should turn the vinegar solution a pinkish color.
5. Then, use the eyedropper to add the baking soda solution to the vinegar until the color changes to purple, indicating a neutral solution.
6. Read the demonstration explanation to the students and have them complete the demonstration sheet on SW p. 91.

Demonstration Explanation

The purpose of this demonstration was for the students to see a neutralization in action. When they are done, read the following to them:

> When an acid and a base are mixed in the right proportions, the resulting solution is neutralized. In the reaction we did, some carbon dioxide was given off. The remaining solution contains only water and a salt (sodium acetate) made from the acid and the base.

{Optional} Take the Demonstration Further

Have the students add drops of vinegar to see if they can turn the solution acidic once more. Then, have them do the same with the baking soda solution to see if they can turn the solution basic.

{Optional} Unit Project

- **Acids and Bases Poster** – This week, the students could add vinegar to the acid poster and baking soda to the base poster. They can simple write the names or they can use pictures.

{Optional} Projects for This Week

- **Fizzy Lemonade** – Let the students have some fun with acids and bases by making some drinkable fizzing lemonade! The directions for this project can be found at the following blog post:
  - https://www.learnwithplayathome.com/2014/09/how-to-make-fizzing-lemonade-edible.html
- **Salt Creation** – Have the students mix a tablespoon of vinegar and a teaspoon of baking soda together on a plate. Then, set the plate in a sunny place and observe what happens over the next several hours. (*The students should see that the liquid evaporates, leaving behind a white powder, which is the salt produced by the reaction, sodium acetate.*)

Write - Notebooking

Writing Assignments

- **Student Workbook** – Have the students dictate, copy, or write two to four sentences on neutralization on SW p. 90.

- ☐ **{Optional} Lapbooking Templates** – Have the students begin the Neutralization sheet on LT p. 50. Have them cut out the sheet and label the pictures "acid", "base", and "water + salt". Then, have them glue the sheet into the lapbook.
- ☐ **{Optional} Coloring Pages** – Have the students color the following pages: Neutralization CP p. 46.

Vocabulary

Have the students look up and copy the definitions for the following words:
- ◊ **Neutralization** – A reaction where one substance fully or partly cancels out another. (SW p. 113)
- ◊ **Salt** – An ionic compound that when dissolved in water makes positive and negative ions. A salt is produced when you combine an acid and a base. (SW p. 117)

{Optional} Weekly Review Sheet

- ✦ "Acids and Bases Weekly Review Sheet 3" on SW p. 165.
    Answers:
    1. Water, salt
    2. True
    3. Ions
    4. Answers will vary

Neutralization

Neutralization is a chemical reaction that happens when an acid and a base cancel one another out. The end result in a neutral solution.

In water, acids like to donate hydrogen ions (H+). On the one hand, bases in water like to donate hydroxide ions (OH-). The two ions are very attracted to each other. The hydrogen ion and the hydroxide ion come together to form something we are very familiar with – water!

There are other ions left in the solution after the acid donates its hydrogen ion and the base donates it hydroxide ion. These ions come together to form a salt.

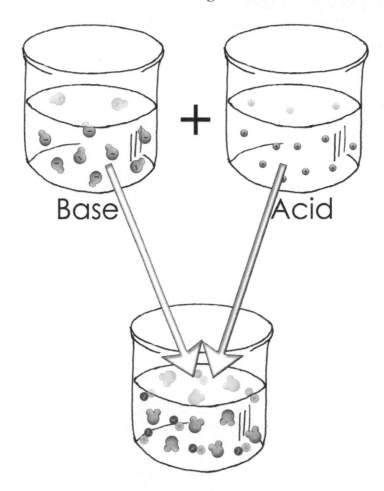

When you mix an acid and a base together in the right proportions, all of the ions will react, and the solution will become neutral.

Week 4: Scientist Biography Lesson Plans

2-Days-a-week Schedule		
	Day 1	Day 2
Read	❏ Read *Who Was Marie Curie?* Prologue to Chapters 4 ❏ {Work on memorizing the "Acids and Bases" poem}	❏ Read *Who Was Marie Curie?* Chapters 5 to 9
Write	❏ Add information about the scientist to the students' Scientist Biography Report Sheet	❏ Add information about the scientist to the students' Scientist Biography Report Sheet ❏ {Work on the Acids and Bases Weekly Review Sheet 4}

5-Days-a-week Schedule					
	Day 1	Day 2	Day 3	Day 4	Day 5
Read	❏ Read *Who Was Marie Curie?* Prologue to Chapter 1	❏ Read *Who Was Marie Curie?* Chapters 2 to 3	❏ Read *Who Was Marie Curie?* Chapters 4 to 5	❏ Read *Who Was Marie Curie?* Chapters 6 to 7	❏ Read *Who Was Marie Curie?* Chapters 8 to 9
Write	❏ Add information about the scientist to the students' Scientist Biography Report Sheet	❏ Add information about the scientist to the students' Scientist Biography Report Sheet	❏ Add information about the scientist to the students' Scientist Biography Report Sheet	❏ Add information about the scientist to the students' Scientist Biography Report Sheet	❏ {Write a written report on the scientist} ❏ {Work on the Acids and Bases Weekly Review Sheet 4}

Read - Information Gathering

Reading Assignment

During this week, the students will read a biography on Marie Curie, a famous scientist who made many discoveries in the field of chemistry, including the element radium. You can purchase the recommended book below, or you can get another book from the library. You can read the book out loud to your students or have them read it on their own. I have included a possible schedule for you with this week's materials.

📖 *Who Was Marie Curie?* by Megan Stine and Nancy Harrison

As you read, have the students tell you what they have learned about Mrs. Curie. You can ask the following questions:

? Who was the scientist you read about?
? When and where was she born?
? What was her major scientific contribution?
? List the events that surround her discovery.
? List some other interesting events in the scientist's life.
? Why do you think that it is important to learn about this scientist?

{Optional} Memory Work

- This week, finish memorizing the "Acids and Bases" poem. (SW p. 125)

Write - Notebooking

Writing Assignments

☐ **Student Workbook** – Have the students fill out the Scientist Biography Report Sheet on SW pp. 92-93.

{Optional} Scientist Biography Report

Once you have completed the book, you can also have the students write a full report on Marie Curie. Have them write a rough draft using their responses on the Scientist Biography Report Sheet. It should include the following:

✓ An introductory paragraph
✓ A paragraph on Curie's scientific contributions
✓ A paragraph on other interesting events in the scientist's life
✓ A conclusion that includes why the students feel it is important to study this particular scientist

After they complete the rough draft, have them proofread and correct mistakes. Finally, have them give their report a title and rewrite it as a final draft. If you want to make the final report a little more interesting, here are two options:

1. Have the students turn their report into a mini-book on the scientist, including pictures they have drawn.
2. Have the students make a poster to present their report.

Chemistry for the Grammar Stage

Organic Chemistry Unit

Organic Chemistry Unit Overview
(4 weeks)

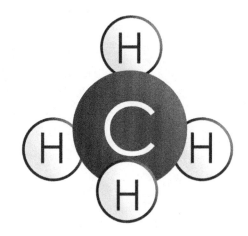

Books Scheduled
- *Usborne Science Encyclopedia*

{Optional Encyclopedias}
- *Basher Science Chemistry*
- *DK Children's Encyclopedia*

Sequence for Study
- Week 1: Organics Compounds
- Week 2: Alcohols and Detergents
- Week 3: Hydrocarbons
- Week 4: Polymers and Plastics

Organic Chemistry Poem to Memorize

<u>Organics</u>
Organic chem is the science of life
Carbon and hydrogen bond without strife
These compounds help keep our bodies stable
But they can be made at the lab table
Alcohols have an OH group to boot
Esters make that sweet taste in gum or fruit
Hydrocarbons are in gas and oil
Polymers create a long-chained coil

Supplies Needed for the Unit

Week	Supplies needed
1	Construction paper, 6 Types of food (Cheese, Fruit, Yogurt, Chips, Muffin, Vegetable), Marker
2	Cotton ball, Vanilla Extract
3	Large clear glass bowl, Vegetable Oil, Water, Plastic spoon, Cotton balls, Polyester felt square
4	Vegetable oil, Cornstarch, Water, Food coloring, Plastic bag, Eyedropper

Unit Vocabulary
1. **Organic Compound** – A compound that contains the element carbon.
2. **Detergent** – A substance that enables water to remove dirt.
3. **Fermentation** – A chemical reaction that breaks down sugar into carbon dioxide and an alcohol.
4. **Polymer** – A substance with long-chain molecules, each made up of many small molecules called monomers.

Week 1: Organics Compounds Lesson Plans

2-Days-a-week Schedule		
	Day 1	**Day 2**
Read	❑ Read "Organic Chemistry, Part 1" ❑ *{Choose one or more of the additional resources to read from this week}*	❑ Read "Organic Chemistry, Part 2" ❑ *{Work on memorizing the "Organics" poem}*
Do	❑ *{Watch the Organic Compounds Video or Do the Fat Warmth Activity}*	❑ Do the Scientific Demonstration: Fat Test
Write	❑ Add information about organic compounds to the students' notebook or lapbook ❑ Define organic compound	❑ Add information about organic compounds to the students' notebook or lapbook ❑ Complete the demonstration sheet ❑ *{Work on the Organic Chemistry Weekly Review Sheet 1}*

5-Days-a-week Schedule					
	Day 1	**Day 2**	**Day 3**	**Day 4**	**Day 5**
Read	❑ Read "Organic Chemistry, Part 1"	❑ Read "Organic Chemistry, Part 2"	❑ *{Work on memorizing the "Organics" poem}*	❑ *{Choose one or more of the additional resources to read from this week}*	❑ *{Choose one or more of the additional resources to read from this week}*
Do	❑ *{Watch the Organic Compounds Video}*	❑ *{Do the Fat Warmth Activity}*	❑ Do the Scientific Demonstration: Fat Test		
Write	❑ Add information about organic compounds to the students' notebook or lapbook	❑ Add information about organic compounds to the students' notebook or lapbook	❑ Complete the demonstration sheet	❑ Define organic compound	❑ *{Work on the Organic Chemistry Weekly Review Sheet 1}*

{These assignments are optional.}

Read – Information Gathering

Reading Assignments

- ❑ *Usborne Science Encyclopedia* p. 92 "Organic Chemistry, Part 1"
    - **?** What are organic compounds?
    - **?** Do you remember where we can find organic compounds?
- ❑ *Usborne Science Encyclopedia* p. 93 "Organic Chemistry, Part 2"
    - **?** What is an unsaturated compound?
    - **?** What is a saturated compound?

{Optional} Memory Work
- This week, begin memorizing the *Organics* poem. (SW p. 126)

{Optional} Additional Resources
Encyclopedias
- *Basher Science Chemistry* p. 68 "Obnoxious Organics,"
- *Usborne Children's Encyclopedia* pp. 114-115 "The Story of Eating"

Library Books
- *Why We Need Fats (Science of Nutrition)* by Molly Aloian
- *Fats for a Healthy Body: For a Healthy Body (Body Needs)* by Heinemann

Do – Demonstration and Activities

Demonstration – Fat Test
You will need the following:
- ✓ Construction paper
- ✓ 6 Types of food (e.g., Cheese, Fruit, Yogurt, Chips, Muffin, Vegetable)
- ✓ Marker

Demonstration Instructions
1. Read the following introduction to the students.

    In this unit, we are going to learn about a special class of chemical compounds called organic compounds. These are compounds that include carbon and other elements, like hydrogen and oxygen. They can be found in living things. In this demonstration, we are going to look for one category of organic compounds called fats.

2. Have the students draw a grid with the marker on the sheet of construction paper. The grid should have six boxes with three across and two down.
3. Have the students set about a tablespoon of each food sample in each of the boxes in the grid and label the box with the type of food. Let the food sit there for 5 to 10 minutes.

4. Then, clean up and dispose of the food samples. Let the paper dry for 30 minutes to an hour.
5. Have the students observe the grid to look for stains that were left behind before completing the demonstration sheet on SW p. 97.

Demonstration Explanation

The purpose of this demonstration was for the students to see that fat is contained in some of the foods we eat. The results for this demonstration will vary, but basically you should see a stain on the paper where a food that contains fat was set. When they are done, read the following to them:

> We saw stains in squares (name the squares). This is because the paper absorbs the fat, and fat does not evaporate like water does.

{Optional} Take the Demonstration Further

Have the students repeat the demonstration with a different group of food items.

{Optional} Unit Project

✂ There is no unit project for this unit.

{Optional} Projects for This Week

✂ **Organic Compounds** – Have the students watch this video to learn the difference between organic and inorganic carbon compounds:
🖱 https://www.youtube.com/watch?v=7fv8GETEOu8

✂ **Fat Warmth** – Have the students see how fats, a type of organic compounds help to keep animals warm. You can get directions of a version of this demonstration here:
🖱 https://www.giftofcuriosity.com/blubber-experiment-how-animals-stay-warm/

Write – Notebooking

Writing Assignments

☐ **Student Workbook** – Have the students dictate, copy, or write two to four sentences on organic compounds on SW p. 96.

☐ **{Optional} Lapbooking Templates** – Have the students begin the Organic Chemistry lapbook by cutting out and coloring the cover on LT p. 52.

☐ **{Optional} Lapbooking Templates** – Have the students begin the Organic Compounds Flap-book on LT pp. 53. Have them cut out the cover and color the picture. Then, have the students cut out the tab for organic compounds and write several sentences on with what they learned about organic compounds for this week. Set the pages aside and save them for completion in week four of this unit.

☐ **{Optional} Coloring Pages** – Have the students color the following pages: Organic Compounds CP p. 47, Detergents CP p. 48.

Vocabulary

Have the students look up and copy the definition for the following word:

✏ **Organic Compound** – A compound that contains the element carbon. (SW p. 114)

{Optional} Weekly Review Sheet

♪ "Organic Chemistry Weekly Review Sheet 1" on SW p. 167.

Answers:
1. Carbon
2. True
3. Detergents
4. Answers will vary

Week 2: Alcohols and Detergents Lesson Plans

2-Days-a-week Schedule		
	Day 1	Day 2
Read	❑ Read "Organic Chemistry, Part 3" ❑ {Choose one or more of the additional resources to read from this week}	❑ Read "Organic Chemistry, Part 4" ❑ {Work on memorizing the "Organics" poem}
Do	❑ {Paint with Alcohol Ink or Make an Ester Solution}	❑ Do the Scientific Demonstration: Scented Alcohol
Write	❑ Add information about alcohol and detergent to the students' notebook or lapbook ❑ Define detergent and fermentation	❑ Add information about esters to the students' notebook or lapbook ❑ Complete the demonstration sheet ❑ {Work on the Organic Chemistry Weekly Review Sheet 2}

5-Days-a-week Schedule					
	Day 1	Day 2	Day 3	Day 4	Day 5
Read	❑ Read "Organic Chemistry, Part 3"	❑ Read "Organic Chemistry, Part 4"	❑ {Work on memorizing the "Organics" poem}	❑ {Choose one or more of the additional resources to read from this week}	❑ {Choose one or more of the additional resources to read from this week}
Do	❑ {Paint with Alcohol Ink}	❑ {Make an Ester Solution}	❑ Do the Scientific Demonstration: Scented Alcohol	❑ {Ferment some bread rolls}	
Write	❑ Add information about alcohol and detergent to the students' notebook or lapbook	❑ Add information about esters to the students' notebook or lapbook	❑ Complete the demonstration sheet	❑ Define detergent and fermentation	❑ {Work on the Organic Chemistry Weekly Review Sheet 2}

Read – Information Gathering

Reading Assignments

- ❑ *Usborne Science Encyclopedia* p. 94 "Organic Chemistry, Part 3"
    - **?** What are alcohols?
    - **?** Can you tell me one way that alcohols are used?
    - **?** Do you remember what happens during fermentation?
- ❑ *Usborne Science Encyclopedia* p. 95 "Organic Chemistry, Part 4"
    - **?** What are esters?
    - **?** Can you tell me one way that esters are used?

{Optional} Memory Work
- This week, begin memorizing the *Organics* poem. (SW p. 126)

{Optional} Additional Resources
Encyclopedias
- *Basher Science Chemistry* p. 72 "Alcohol," p. 76 "Esters"

Library Books
There are no additional books on the market for these topics. Instead, you can watch the following video on fermentation:
- The Chemistry of Bread: https://www.youtube.com/watch?v=qylxpwNhFYI

Do – Demonstration and Activities

Demonstration – Scented Alcohol
You will need the following:
- ✓ Cotton ball
- ✓ Vanilla extract (or any other food-grade extract)

Demonstration Instructions
1. Read the following introduction to the students.

    Last week, we learned about organic compounds. Alcohols are organic compounds that contain carbon, hydrogen, and oxygen. These chemical compounds are often used in industry, including in making perfumes and extracts. In this demonstration, we are going to see how alcohol can carry a scent.

2. Put several drops of vanilla extract on the cotton ball.
3. Have the students wipe the cotton ball on the back of their hand and let it dry.
4. Then, have them smell the back of their hand and note their observation on the demonstration sheet on SW p. 99.

5. Read the demonstration explanation to the students and have them complete the demonstration sheet.

Demonstration Explanation

The purpose of this demonstration was for the students to see help the students see how alcohol can carry a scent. When they are done, read the following to them:

> We still could smell the vanilla on your hand even after the spot dried. Alcohol is known to dissolve aromatic compounds, like vanilla and other flavors used in extracts. When the vanilla extract is placed on your skin, the alcohol evaporates and leaves behind the scent of vanilla.

{Optional} Take the Demonstration Further

Have the students create their own perfume using a concoction of different spices, dried herbs, or dried flowers.

{Optional} Projects for This Week

- **Alcohols –** Have the students use alcohol ink to paint on a slick surface, such as tile or glass. There are several ideas for this type of project in the following post:
  https://truebluemeandyou.com/post/128038875325/diy-alcohol-ink-glasses
  Note – *You can make your own alcohol ink by mixing a teaspoon of liquid dye, such as RIT dye, and a quarter of a cup of isopropyl alcohol.*
- **Fermentation –** Have the students use fermentation to make some fluffy rolls! Any recipe for yeast rolls will work, including the one found on the back of the yeast package.
- **Ester Solution –** Have the students make an ester. You will need ethanol (denatured alcohol), sodium bisulfate (can be found at store that carries pool or wine-making supplies), and vinegar. Mix 3 teaspoons of ethanol with 2 teaspoons of sodium bisulfate. Then, add 3 teaspoons of vinegar and carefully smell the solution. (*The vinegar should have been replaced with the fruity scent of the ester that was made, ethyl acetate.*) **CAUTION –** Do not drink or touch the solution. When you dispose of the solution, be sure to flush it down with plenty of water.

Write – Notebooking

Writing Assignments

- ☐ **Student Workbook –** Have the students dictate, copy, or write two to four sentences on alcohols and detergents on SW p. 98.
- ☐ **{Optional} Lapbooking Templates –** Have the students work on the Organic Compounds Flap-book on LT p. 55. Have them cut out the sheet for alcohols and write several sentences on with what they learned about alcohols for this week. Set the pages aside and save them for completion in week four of this unit.
- ☐ **{Optional} Lapbooking Templates –** Have the students complete the Esters Mini-book on LT p. 59. Have the students cut out and fold the template. Have them color the picture

on the cover. Then, have the students write several sentences about what they have learned. Finally, glue the mini-book into the lapbook.
- ☐ **{Optional} Lapbooking Templates** – Have the students complete the Detergents Mini-book on LT p. 58. Have the students cut out and fold the template. Have them color the picture on the cover. Then, have the students several sentences about what they have learned. Finally, glue the mini-book into the lapbook.
- ☐ **{Optional} Coloring Pages** – Have the students color the following pages: Alcohols CP p. 49, Esters CP p. 50.

Vocabulary

Have the students look up and copy the definitions for the following words:
- ↻ **Detergent** – A substance that enables water to remove dirt. (SW p. 109)
- ↻ **Fermentation** – A chemical reaction that breaks down sugar into carbon dioxide and an alcohol. (SW p. 111)

{Optional} Weekly Review Sheet

- ✦ "Organic Chemistry Weekly Review Sheet 2" on SW p. 168.

    Answers:
    1. Carbon, Hydrogen, Oxygen
    2. False (*Fermentation is a chemical reaction that produces alcohol.*)
    3. Smell
    4. Answers will vary

Week 3: Hydrocarbons Lesson Plans

	2-Days-a-week Schedule	
	Day 1	**Day 2**
Read	❏ Read "Crude Oil, Part 1" ❏ {Choose one or more of the additional resources to read from this week}	❏ Read "Crude Oil, Part 2" ❏ {Work on memorizing the "Organics" poem}
Do	❏ Do the Scientific Demonstration: Oily Clean-up	❏ {Do the Oil Spill activity or Watch the Accidental Discoveries Video}
Write	❏ Add information about hydrocarbons to the students' notebook or lapbook ❏ Complete the demonstration sheet	❏ Add information about hydrocarbons to the students' notebook or lapbook ❏ {Work on the Organic Chemistry Weekly Review Sheet 3}

	5-Days-a-week Schedule				
	Day 1	**Day 2**	**Day 3**	**Day 4**	**Day 5**
Read	❏ Read "Crude Oil, Part 1"	❏ Read "Crude Oil, Part 2"	❏ {Work on memorizing the "Organics" poem}	❏ {Choose one or more of the additional resources to read from this week}	❏ {Choose one or more of the additional resources to read from this week}
Do	❏ {Do the Oil Spill activity}		❏ Do the Scientific Demonstration: Oily Clean-up	❏ {Watch the Accidental Discoveries Video}	
Write	❏ Add information about hydrocarbons to the students' notebook or lapbook	❏ Add information about hydrocarbons to the students' notebook or lapbook	❏ Complete the demonstration sheet		❏ {Work on the Organic Chemistry Weekly Review Sheet 3}

Read – Information Gathering

Reading Assignments

❑ *Usborne Science Encyclopedia* p. 98 "Crude Oil, Part 1"
  ? What is crude oil?
  ? Do you remember how oil and gas are made?

❑ *Usborne Science Encyclopedia* p. 99 "Crude Oil, Part 2"
  ? What is fractional distillation?
  ? Can you name several of the compounds that can be made from crude oil?

{Optional} Memory Work

- This week, begin memorizing the *Organics* poem. (SW p. 126)

{Optional} Additional Resources

Encyclopedias
  📖 *Basher Science Chemistry* p. 70 "Hydrocarbon"
  📖 *DK Children's Encyclopedia* p. 97 "Fossil Fuels"

Library Books
  📖 *Oil Spill! (Let's-Read-and-Find-Out Science)* by Melvin Berger and Paul Mirocha
  📖 *Using Coal, Oil, and Gas (Exploring Earth's Resources)* by Sharon Katz Cooper
  📖 *From Oil to Gas (Start to Finish, Second Series: Everyday Products)* by Shannon Zemlicka
  📖 *Finding Out About Coal, Oil, and Natural Gas* by Matt Doeden

Do – Demonstration and Activities

Demonstration – Oily Clean-up

You will need the following:
- ✓ Large clear glass bowl
- ✓ Vegetable Oil
- ✓ Water
- ✓ Plastic spoon
- ✓ Cotton balls
- ✓ Polyester felt square

Demonstration Instructions

1. Read the following introduction to the students.

   Last week, we learned about alcohols and detergents. This week we are looking at other group of organic compounds, hydrocarbons. Hydrocarbons include the oil and gas we use to power modern machinery. In this demonstration, we are going to look at how to clean up a hydrocarbon spill.

2. Fill the bowl a halfway with water and add a half of a cup of oil to create a layer of oil sitting on top of the water.
3. Have the students choose one of the materials (spoon, cotton balls, or polyester felt) with which to soak or scoop up the oil. Have them record the results of their efforts on the demonstration sheet on SW p. 101.
4. Then, have the students repeat the procedure from step 2 with the remaining two materials.
5. After they are done, read the demonstration explanation to the students and have them complete the demonstration sheet.

Demonstration Explanation

The purpose of this demonstration was for the students to see what materials can be used to clean up an oil spill. When they are done, read the following to them:

> We saw that the plastic spoon and polyester felt worked the best to clean up the oil. This is because both these materials are attracted to the oil, given that they are also non-polar, and they allow you to scoop up the oil rather than dab it away.

{Optional} Take the Demonstration Further

Have the students make a polypropylene scoop and then repeat the demonstration. To make the boom cleaner, you will need a polypropylene cloth sock or glove liners and a bit of wire. Use the wire to create a stiff "O" at the opening of the sock or glove liner. Then, use the scoop you have created to clean up the oil. (*This scoop is very similar to the boom-cleaner used to clean up large scale oil spills in the environment.*)

{Optional} Projects for This Week

✄ **Oil Spill** - Have the students learn the effects oil spills have on animals. You will need two feathers, vegetable oil, water, and dish soap for this activity. Begin by having the students dip the two feathers into the oil to coat them completely. Then, have them try to rinse the oil off one of the feathers with just water. Next, have them rub a bit of dish soap on the other feather until it lathers up. Then, rinse that feather off with water. Set both feathers on a paper towel to dry. After about an hour, observe the changes to see which feather had the most oil removed from it. (*The students should see that the feather that was washed with the dish soap had the most oil removed. This is because the soap captures more of the oil so that it can be removed by the water.*)

✄ **Accidental Discoveries Video** - Have the students watch the following video about accidental discoveries relating to coal tar, a byproduct of crude oil, and other hydrocarbons:
   https://www.youtube.com/watch?v=Xowen_a787Y

Write - Notebooking

Writing Assignments
- ☐ **Student Workbook** – Have the students dictate, copy, or write two to four sentences on hydrocarbons on SW p. 100.
- ☐ **{Optional} Lapbooking Templates** – Have the students work on the Organic Compounds Flap-book on LT p. 56. Have them cut out the sheet for hydrocarbons and write several sentences on with what they learned about hydrocarbons for this week. Set the pages aside and save them for completion in week four of this unit.
- ☐ **{Optional} Coloring Pages** – Have the students color the following page: Hydrocarbons CP p. 51.

Vocabulary
There are no vocabulary words for this week.

{Optional} Weekly Review Sheet
- "Organic Chemistry Weekly Review Sheet 3" on SW p. 168.
    Answers:
    1. True
    2. All the chemicals should be circled.
    3. Fractional distillation
    4. Answers will vary

Week 4: Polymers and Plastics Lesson Plans

2-Days-a-week Schedule		
	Day 1	Day 2
Read	☐ Read "Polymers and Plastics, Part 1" ☐ {Choose one or more of the additional resources to read from this week}	☐ Read "Polymers and Plastics, Part 2" ☐ {Work on memorizing the "Organics" poem}
Do	☐ {Make a Polymer Slime or Go on a Plastic Hunt}	☐ Do the Scientific Demonstration: Kitchen Plastic
Write	☐ Add information about polymers to the students' notebook or lapbook ☐ Define polymer	☐ Add information about plastics to the students' notebook or lapbook ☐ Complete the demonstration sheet ☐ {Work on the Organic Chemistry Weekly Review Sheet 4}

5-Days-a-week Schedule					
	Day 1	Day 2	Day 3	Day 4	Day 5
Read	☐ Read "Polymers and Plastics, Part 1"	☐ Read "Polymers and Plastics, Part 2"	☐ {Work on memorizing the "Organics" poem}	☐ {Choose one or more of the additional resources to read from this week}	☐ {Choose one or more of the additional resources to read from this week}
Do	☐ {Make a Polymer Slime}	☐ {Go on a Plastic Hunt}	☐ Do the Scientific Demonstration: Kitchen Plastic		
Write	☐ Add information about polymers to the students' notebook or lapbook	☐ Add information about plastics to the students' notebook or lapbook	☐ Complete the demonstration sheet	☐ Define polymer	☐ {Work on the Organic Chemistry Weekly Review Sheet 4}

Read – Information Gathering

Reading Assignments

❑ *Usborne Science Encyclopedia* p. 101 "Polymers and Plastics, Part 1"
- **?** What are polymers?
- **?** Can you tell me what the difference is between synthetic and natural polymers?
- **?** What is polymerization?

❑ *Usborne Science Encyclopedia* p. 102 "Polymers and Plastics, Part 2"
- **?** What are the two groups of plastics?
- **?** Do you remember what plastics can be used for?

{Optional} Memory Work
- This week, begin memorizing the *Organics* poem. (SW p. 126)

{Optional} Additional Resources

Encyclopedias
- *Basher Science Chemistry* p. 35 "Polymer"
- *DK Children's Encyclopedia* p. 190 "Plastic"

Library Books
- *Plastic (Everyday Materials)* by Andrew Langley
- *Plastic, Ahoy!: Investigating the Great Pacific Garbage Patch* by Patricia Newman and Annie Crawley
- *The Adventures of a Plastic Bottle: A Story About Recycling (Little Green Books)* by Alison Inches and Pete Whitehead
- *From Plastic to Soccer Ball (Start to Finish: Sports Gear)* by Robin Nelson

Do – Demonstration and Activities

Demonstration – Kitchen Plastic

You will need the following:
- ✓ Vegetable oil
- ✓ Cornstarch
- ✓ Water
- ✓ Food coloring
- ✓ Plastic bag
- ✓ Eyedropper

Demonstration Instructions

1. Read the following introduction to the students.

Last week, we learned about hydrocarbons. This week we are going to look at polymers and plastics. These compounds make up many of the things we use today, such as styrofoam containers, plastic wrap, and synthetic fibers used in clothing. In this demonstration, we are going to make our own plastic using items from our kitchen!

2. In the bag, mix 3 tablespoons of cornstarch, 3 tablespoons of water, 8 to 10 drops of vegetable oil, and a few drops of food coloring.
3. Have the students mix the ingredients up thoroughly.
4. Then, seal the bag halfway, place it on a plate, and place the bag in the microwave on high for 25 to 30 seconds. *(The mixture should bubble a bit and become somewhat transparent.)*
5. Use a hot mitt to remove the bag and let it cool for a bit.
6. Once it is cool enough to handle, you can shape the plastic into what the students desire. Then, let it sit overnight to completely harden.
7. Read the demonstration explanation to the students and have them complete the demonstration sheet on SW p. 103.

Demonstration Explanation

The purpose of this demonstration was for the students to see that they can make a plastic from the materials in your kitchen. When they are done, read the following to them:

We created a soft moldable plastic that hardens if we leave it overnight. In the demonstration, as the cornstarch heated up, it reacted with the water and oil to create a polymer, which is the basic unit of plastic materials.

{Optional} Take the Demonstration Further

Have the students make a different kind of bioplastic using milk and vinegar. The directions for this can be found at the following website:
  https://sciencebob.com/make-plastic-milk/

{Optional} Projects for This Week

- **Polymer Slime** – Have the students make their own polymer slime. You will need white (or clear gel) glue, water, a plastic bag, and some Borax (the laundry booster, not the laundry detergent.) Begin by mixing 4 oz. of glue with 4 oz. of water in a plastic bag. Next, in a separate cup, mix a quarter cup of water with half a teaspoon of Borax. Add the Borax solution to the bag and massage the bag for a few minutes until a nice firm slime has formed. Then, pull the slime out of the bag and let the students have fun with their polymer.
- **Plastic Hunt** – Have the students go on a hunt around the house to find what items are made of plastic. Then, have them create a collage displaying their results. They can draw, cut out, or take and paste pictures of the items they find.

Write - Notebooking

Writing Assignments
- [ ] **Student Workbook** – Have the students dictate, copy, or write two to four sentences on polymers and plastics on SW p. 102.
- [ ] **{Optional} Lapbooking Templates** – Have the students work on the Organic Compounds Flap-book on LT p. 57. Have them cut out the sheet for polymers and write several sentences on with what they learned about polymers for this week. Set the pages aside and save them for completion in week four of this unit.
- [ ] **{Optional} Lapbooking Templates** – Have the students finish their lapbook. Have them cut out and color the *Organics* poem on LT p. 60. Once they are done, have them glue the sheet into their lapbook.
- [ ] **{Optional} Coloring Pages** – Have the students color the following pages: Polymer CP p. 52, Plastic CP p. 53.

Vocabulary
Have the students look up and copy the definition for the following word:
- **Polymer** – A substance with long-chain molecules, each made up of many small molecules called monomers. (SW p. 115)

{Optional} Weekly Review Sheet
- "Organic Chemistry Weekly Review Sheet 4" on SW p. 170.
    Answers:
    1. Short
    2. True
    3. Man
    4. Answers will vary

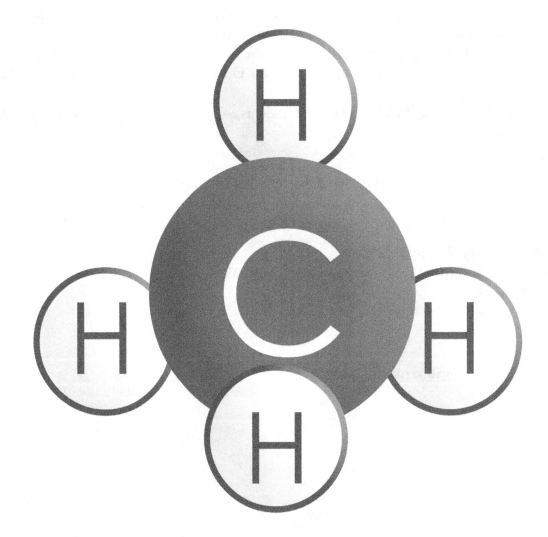

Chemistry for the Grammar Stage

Appendix

Transition Metal Hunt

21 **Sc** Scandium 44.96	22 **Ti** Titanium 47.87	23 **V** Vanadium 50.94	24 **Cr** Chromium 52.00	25 **Mn** Manganese 54.94	26 **Fe** Iron 55.85	27 **Co** Cobalt 58.93	28 **Ni** Nickel 58.69	29 **Cu** Copper 63.55	30 **Zn** Zinc 65.39
39 **Y** Yttrium 88.91	40 **Zr** Zirconium 91.22	41 **Nb** Niobium 92.91	42 **Mo** Molybdenum 95.94	43 **Tc** Technetium 98.91	44 **Ru** Ruthenium 101.1	45 **Rh** Rhodium 102.9	46 **Pd** Palladium 106.4	47 **Ag** Silver 107.9	48 **Cd** Cadmium 112.4
* 71 **Lu** Lutetium 175.0	72 **Hf** Hafnium 178.5	73 **Ta** Tantalum 181.0	74 **W** Tungsten 183.9	75 **Re** Rhenium 186.2	76 **Os** Osmium 190.2	77 **Ir** Iridium 192.2	78 **Pt** Platinum 195.1	79 **Au** Gold 197.0	80 **Hg** Mercury 200.6

Many of the transition metals can be found in your house! Today, you are going to hunt around your home looking for some of the elements above. You can look anywhere you have permission to do so. (*Be sure to check the labels in your pantry and medicine cabinet as well!*) Here are a few ideas of items you can look for:

- ✓ Jewelry, which is often made from gold, silver, or platinum.
- ✓ Coins, which contain copper and nickel.
- ✓ Stainless steel, which is combination of iron, vanadium, nickel, tungsten, and more.
- ✓ Magnets are usually made from iron.
- ✓ Antiperspirant contains zirconium.
- ✓ Lightbulb filaments are made from tungsten.
- ✓ Bicycle frames are sometimes made of titanium.
- ✓ Anything with Vitamin B12, which contains colbalt.
- ✓ Fishing lures, which often contain lead.
- ✓ Hand tools are often coated with chrom-moly steel, which contains chromium and molybdenum.
- ✓ Diaper cream often contains zinc.
- ✓ Rechargeable batteries can contain both nickel and cadmium.

Project Record Sheet

Paste a picture of your project in this box.

What I Learned:

_____
_____
_____
_____
_____
_____
_____

Chemistry for the Grammar Stage Teacher Guide ~ Appendix Templates

Two Days a Week Schedule

Day 1	Day 2
❑	❑
❑	❑
❑	❑
❑	❑
❑	❑
❑	❑

Things to Prepare

❑

❑

❑

Notes

Five Days a Week Schedule

Day 1	Day 2	Day 3	Day 4	Day 5
☐	☐	☐	☐	☐
☐	☐	☐	☐	☐
☐	☐	☐	☐	☐
☐	☐	☐	☐	☐

All Week Long

☐

☐

Things to Prepare

☐

☐

☐

Notes

Chemistry for the Grammar Stage

Glossary

A

- **Acid** – A chemical that dissolves in water and can neutralize a base. Weak acids taste sour.
- **Air** – A mixture of gases that forms a protective layer around the Earth.
- **Alloy** – A mixture of two or more metals or a metal and a nonmetal.
- **Atomic Mass** – The average mass number of the atoms in a sample of an element.
- **Atomic Number** – The number of protons in the nucleus of an atom.

B

- **Base** – A chemical that dissolves in water and can neutralize an acid. Weak bases taste bitter.

C

- **Catalyst** – A substance that speeds up a chemical reaction.
- **Chemical Bond** – A force that holds together two or more atoms.
- **Chemical Reaction** – An occurrence where the atoms in substances are rearranged to form new substances.
- **Chemical Symbol** – A shorthand way of representing a specific element in formulae and equations.
- **Chromatography** – A method of separating the substances in a mixture by the rate they move through or along a medium, such as filter paper.
- **Crystal** – A solid substance with a definite geometrical shape, straight edges and flat surfaces; hard, glassy-looking objects made of minerals.

D

- **Detergent** – A substance that enables water to remove dirt.
- **Diffusion** – The spreading out of a gas to fill the available space.

E

- **Electron** – A negatively charged particle in an atom.
- **Electron Shell** – The region around an atom's nucleus in which a certain number of electrons can reside.

- **Elements** – A substance made up of one type of atom, which cannot be broken down by chemical reaction to form a simpler substance.
- **Enzyme** – A catalyst that speeds up a chemical reaction in living things.
- **Essential Element** – An element that is essential to life on earth, such as carbon, hydrogen, nitrogen, or oxygen.
- **Evaporation** – The process by which the surface molecules of a liquid escape into a vapor.

F

- **Fermentation** – A chemical reaction that breaks down sugar into carbon dioxide and an alcohol.

G

H

- **Hard Water** – Water that contains a lot of dissolved minerals.

I

- **Indicator** – A substance that changes color in the presence of an acid or base.
- **Inert** – An element that is completely nonreactive.
- **Ion** – An atom or group of atoms that has become charged by gaining or losing one or more electrons.
- **Isotope** – An atom that has a different number of neutrons and so has a different mass number from the other atoms of an element.

J

K

L

M

- **Metal** – The largest class of elements; they are usually shiny and solid at room temperature.

- **Metalloid** – An element that shares some of the properties of metals and nonmetals.
- **Mixture** – A combination of two or more elements that are not chemically bonded together.
- **Molecule** – A substance made up of two or more atoms that are chemically bonded.

N

- **Neutralization** – A reaction where one substance fully or partly cancels out another.
- **Neutron** – A neutral particle in an atom.
- **Nonmetal** – A class of elements that can be nonshiny solids or gases.

O

- **Organic Compound** – A compound that contains the element carbon.
- **Oxidation** – A chemical reaction in which a substance combines with oxygen.

P

- **Periodic Table** – A systematic arrangement of the elements in order of increasing atomic number.
- **pH** – A scale from 0 to 14 used to measure the strength of acids and bases.
- **Physical Change** – A change that occurs in which no new substances are made.
- **Polymer** – A substance with long-chain molecules, each made up of many small molecules called monomers.
- **Proton** – A positively charged particle in an atom.

Q

R

- **Radioactive Decay** – The process by which a nucleus ejects particles through radiation to become the nucleus of a series of different elements until stability is reached.
- **Reactive** – The tendency of a substance to react with other substances.
- **Redox Reaction** – A chemical reaction that involves the transfer of electrons.
- **Refraction** – The bending of light as it passes through a different medium.

S

- **Salt** – An ionic compound that when dissolved in water makes positive and negative ions. A salt is produced when you combine an acid and a base.

- **Solution** – A mixture that consists of a substance dissolved in a liquid.

- **States of Matter** – The different forms in which a substance can exist: solid, liquid, and gas.

- **Sublimation** – A change from solid to gas without going through liquid form.

- **Surface Tension** – A force that pulls together molecules on the surface of a liquid.

T

U

V

- **Volume** – The space occupied by matter.

W

X

Y

Z

Chemistry for the Grammar Stage

Additional Library Book List

Additional Books Listed by Week

The books listed below are completely optional! They are not required to complete this program. Instead, this list is merely a suggestion of the additional books that are available to enhance your studies. This list is by no means exhaustive.

Atoms and Molecules Unit

Atoms and Molecules Week 1
- *What Are Atoms? (Rookie Read-About Science)* by Lisa Trumbauer
- *Atoms and Molecules (Building Blocks of Matter)* by Richard and Louise Spilsbury
- *Atoms (Simply Science)* by Melissa Stewart

Atoms and Molecules Week 2
- *Atoms and Molecules (Building Blocks of Matter)* by Richard and Louise Spilsbury
- *Atoms and Molecules (Why Chemistry Matters)* by Molly Aloian
- *Atoms and Molecules (My Science Library)* by Tracy Nelson Maurer

Atoms and Molecules Week 3
- *Air Is All Around You (Let's-Read-and-Find... Science 1)* by Franklyn M. Branley
- *Air: Outside, Inside, and All Around (Amazing Science)* by Darlene R. Stille

Atoms and Molecules Week 4
- *Water, Water Everywhere (Reading Rainbow Book)* by Cynthia Overbeck Bix
- *Water* by Frank Asch
- *Water: Up, Down, and All Around (Amazing Science)* by Natalie M. Rosinsky

Periodic Table Unit

Periodic Table Week 1
- *The Elements (True Books)* by Matt Mullins
- *Elements and Compounds (Building Blocks of Matter)* by Louise and Richard Spilsbury
- *The Mystery of the Periodic Table (Living History Library)* by Benjamin D. Wiker, Jeanne Bendick and Theodore Schluenderfritz
- *The Periodic Table (True Books: Elements)* by Salvatore Tocci

Periodic Table Week 2
- *The Alkali Metals: Lithium, Sodium, Potassium, Rubidium, Cesium, Francium (Understanding the Elements of the Periodic Table)* by Kristi Lew
- *Hydrogen and the Noble Gases (True Books: Elements)* by Salvatore Tocci
- *Hydrogen: Running on Water (Energy Revolution)* by Niki Walker
- *Sodium (Elements)* by Anne O'Daly
- *Sodium (True Books: Elements)* by Salvatore Tocci

Periodic Table Week 3
- 📖 *The Alkaline Earth Metals: Beryllium, Magnesium, Calcium, Strontium, Barium, Radium (Understanding the Elements of the Periodic Table)* by Bridget Heos
- 📖 *Calcium (True Books: Elements)* by Salvatore Tocci
- 📖 *Magnesium (The Elements)* by Colin Uttley

Periodic Table Week 4
- 📖 *The Transition Elements: The 37 Transition Metals (Understanding the Elements of the Periodic Table)* by Mary-Lane Kamberg
- 📖 *Iron (Elements)* by Giles Sparrow
- 📖 *Copper (The Elements)* by Richard Beatty

Periodic Table Week 5
- 📖 *The Boron Elements: Boron, Aluminum, Gallium, Indium, Thallium (Understanding the Elements of the Periodic Table)* by Heather Hasan
- 📖 *Aluminum* by Heather Hasan
- 📖 *Boron (Elements)* by Richard Beatty

Periodic Table Week 6
- 📖 *The Carbon Elements: Carbon, Silicon, Germanium, Tin, Lead (Understanding the Elements of the Periodic Table)* by Brian Belval
- 📖 *Carbon* by Linda Saucerman
- 📖 *Carbon (True Books: Elements)* by Salvatore Tocci
- 📖 *Tin (True Books: Elements)* by Salvatore Tocci
- 📖 *The Invention of the Silicon Chip: A Revolution in Daily Life* by Windsor Chorlton

Periodic Table Week 7
- 📖 *The Nitrogen Elements (Understanding the Elements of the Periodic Table)* by Greg Roza
- 📖 *Nitrogen (True Books: Elements)* by Salvatore Tocci
- 📖 *Nitrogen* by Heather Hasan
- 📖 *Phosphorus (Elements)* by Richard Beatty

Periodic Table Week 8
- 📖 *The Oxygen Elements: Oxygen, Sulfur, Selenium, Tellurium, Polonium (Understanding the Elements of the Periodic Table)* by Laura La Bella
- 📖 *Nonmetals (Material Matters/Freestyle Express)* by Carol Baldwin
- 📖 *Oxygen (True Books: Elements)* by Salvatore Tocci
- 📖 *Sulfur (The Elements)* by Richard Beatty

Periodic Table Week 9
- 📖 *Fluorine (Understanding the Elements of the Periodic Table)* by Heather Hasan
- 📖 *The Elements: Iodine* by Leon Gray
- 📖 *Iodine (Understanding the Elements of the Periodic Table)* by Kristi Lew

Periodic Table Week 10
- 📖 *Hydrogen and the Noble Gases (True Books: Elements)* by Salvatore Tocci
- 📖 *Krypton (Understanding the Elements of the Periodic Table)* by Janey Levy

Periodic Table Week 11
- 📖 *The Lanthanides (Elements)* by Richard Beatty

Periodic Table Week 12
- 📖 *Radioactive Elements* by Tom Jackson
- 📖 *The 15 Lanthanides and the 15 Actinides (Understanding the Elements of the Periodic Table)* by Kristi Lew

Physical Changes Unit

Physical Changes Week 1
- 📖 *What Is the World Made Of? All About Solids, Liquids, and Gases (Let's-Read-and-Find... Science, Stage 2)* by Kathleen Weidner Zoehfeld and Paul Meisel
- 📖 *Solids, Liquids, And Gases (Rookie Read-About Science)* by Ginger Garrett
- 📖 *States of Matter: A Question and Answer Book* by Fiona Bayrock and Anne McMullen

Physical Changes Week 2
- 📖 *How Water Changes (Weekly Reader: Science)* by Jim Mezzanotte
- 📖 *Solids (States of Matter)* by Jim Mezzanotte
- 📖 *Liquids (States of Matter)* by Jim Mezzanotte
- 📖 *Gases (States of Matter)* Jim Mezzanotte

Physical Changes Week 3
- 📖 *What Is a Liquid?* (First Step Nonfiction, States of Matter) by Jennifer Boothroyd
- 📖 *How Do You Measure Liquids?* (A+ Books: Measure It!) by Thomas K. Adamson
- 📖 *Saving Water: The Water Cycle* (Do It Yourself) by Buffy Silverman
- 📖 *Why Do Puddles Disappear?: Noticing Forms of Water* by Martha E. H. Rustad and Christine M. Schneider

Physical Changes Week 4
- 📖 *What Is a Gas? (First Step Nonfiction)* by Jennifer Boothroyd
- 📖 *It's a Gas!* by Ruth Griffin, Margaret Griffin and Pat Cupples
- 📖 *The Atmosphere: Planetary Heat Engine (Earth's Spheres)*

Chemical Changes Unit

There are no additional books for this unit, instead there are suggested videos for the topics.

Chemistry for the Grammar Stage Teacher Guide ~ Additional Library Book List

Mixtures Unit

Mixtures Week 1
- *Compounds and Mixtures (Explorer Library: Science Explorer)* by Charnan Simon
- *Mixtures and Solutions (Why Chemistry Matters)* by Molly Aloian
- *Mix It Up! Solution or Mixture?* by Tracy Nelson Maurer
- *Mixtures and Solutions (Building Blocks of Matter)* by Richard Spilsbury and Louise Spilsbury

Mixtures Week 2
- *Mixing and Separating (Changing Materials)* by Chris Oxlade
- *Mixtures and Compounds (Internet-linked Library of Science)* by Alastair Smith and P. Clarke

Mixtures Week 3
- *Crystals (Rocks and Minerals)* by Connor Dayton
- *Growing Crystals* by Ann O Squire
- *What Are Crystals? (Let's Rock!)* by Molly Aloian
- *DK Eyewitness Books: Crystal & Gem* by R.F. Symes

Mixtures Week 4
- *Louis Pasteur: Founder of Modern Medicine* by John Hudson Tiner and Michael L. Denman
- *Germ Hunter: A Story about Louis Pasteur* by Elaine Marie Alphin and Elaine Verstraete
- *Louis Pasteur and the Fight Against Germs: Life Science* by Lisa Zamosky
- *Louis Pasteur: The Father of Microbiology* by Stephen Feinstein

Acids and Bases Unit

Acids and Bases Week 1
- *Acids and Bases (Why Chemistry Matters)* by Lynnette Brent
- *Acids & Bases (Material Matters)* by Carol Baldwin
- *Acids and Bases (Chemicals in Action)* by Chris Oxlade

Acids and Bases Week 2
- There are no additional books for this unit, instead there are suggested videos for the topics.

Acids and Bases Week 3
- *From Sea to Salt (Start to Finish, Second Series)* by Lisa Owings
- *The Story of Salt* by Mark Kurlansky and S. D. Schindler

Acids and Bases Week 4
- 📖 *Who Was Marie Curie?* by Megan Stine and Nancy Harrison
- 📖 *DK Biography: Marie Curie* by DK
- 📖 *Marie Curie (Giants of Science)* by Kathleen Krull
- 📖 *World History Biographies: Marie Curie: The Woman Who Changed the Course of Science* by Philip Steele

Organic Chemistry Unit

Organic Chemistry Week 1
- 📖 *Why We Need Fats (Science of Nutrition)* by Molly Aloian
- 📖 *Fats for a Healthy Body: For a Healthy Body (Body Needs)* by Heinemann

Organic Chemistry Week 2
- 📖 There are no additional books for this unit, instead there are suggested videos for the topics.

Organic Chemistry Week 3
- 📖 *Oil Spill! (Let's-Read-and-Find-Out Science)* by Melvin Berger and Paul Mirocha
- 📖 *Using Coal, Oil, and Gas (Exploring Earth's Resources)* by Sharon Katz Cooper
- 📖 *From Oil to Gas (Start to Finish, Second Series: Everyday Products)* by Shannon Zemlicka
- 📖 *Finding Out About Coal, Oil, and Natural Gas* by Matt Doeden

Organic Chemistry Week 4
- 📖 *Plastic (Everyday Materials)* by Andrew Langley
- 📖 *Plastic, Ahoy!: Investigating the Great Pacific Garbage Patch* by Patricia Newman and Annie Crawley
- 📖 *The Adventures of a Plastic Bottle: A Story About Recycling (Little Green Books)* by Alison Inches and Pete Whitehead
- 📖 *From Plastic to Soccer Ball (Start to Finish: Sports Gear)* by Robin Nelson

Made in the USA
Monee, IL
06 September 2024